"*Parenting without God* is not just about the absence of religion—it's about the glorious space that opens up for secular parents and their lucky kids once the clutter and smoke of religion is gone. Dan Arel's voice is clear, smart, and a welcome addition to the growing chorus of parents taking the hands of their children and running at full speed into the real world."
—Dale McGowan, author/editor of *Parenting Beyond Belief* and *Raising Freethinkers*

"If *Parenting without God* has a central message, it is that knowing what you are not going to do isn't a plan. For children to succeed, parents must offer them a better, truer view of history, the universe, morality, and themselves. Arel's book from beginning to end and is, I believe, what truly differentiates the secular ideal from the rigid prescriptions of religious parenting."
—M. Dolon Hickman, author of *13:24: A Story of Faith and Obsession*

D0710927

Parenting without God

Dan Arel

Parenting without God
Dan Arel
© 2019 Dan Arel
Introduction © 2019 Jessica Mills
This edition © 2019 PM Press

ISBN: 978-1-62963-708-2

Library of Congress Control Number: 2019933017

Cover by John Yates / www.stealworks.com
Interior design by briandesign

10 9 8 7 6 5 4 3 2 1

PM Press
PO Box 23912
Oakland, CA 94623
www.pmpress.org

Printed in the USA.

Contents

Foreword

by Jessica Mills

Parenting with God never crossed our minds. Neither my partner nor I came from particularly religious families, and our desire to raise freethinking children also had everything to do with the fact that we never had a conversation along the lines of "Are we going to impose religious dogma on our kids?" We were old enough to have learned by then the baggage that comes with that kind of imposition, and we were young enough not to consider how our religion-free kids may find themselves at odds with the deeply religious country around them.

My parents did not attend church, but my mom did send me to Sunday school with my GrandMary so I could learn "the morals." I only attended on holidays and during summers, because until I was twelve I did not live in the same city as my GrandMary. She was a woman of deep faith, eventually becoming the first reader of the Church of Christ, Scientist in Daytona Beach, Florida. Christian Science services have no clergy, sermons, or rituals, and they perform no baptisms, marriages, or burials, but they do read aloud "lessons" from both the Bible and *Science and Health with Key to the Scriptures* (Christian Science's central texts), sing hymns from the *Christian Science Hymnal*, and offer testimonials about metaphysical "healings" and gratitude. Though I did appreciate the testimonials of gratitude, I found the rest of the services and Sunday school mind-numbing. I loathed sitting around talking and listening to their religious ideas, which I really didn't understand, and because it's a cult religion that's been experiencing a decline in membership since the 1940s, I was sometimes the only kid in the class. It's no wonder I didn't really get anything out of it, because the lessons were not reinforced at home. Until I was in sixth grade, I didn't even realize that Christian Scientists didn't use doctors. I mean, I knew it was a weird, small church, and that my mom's younger brother had died when he was a toddler because of the family not seeking medical attention when he needed it, but not until a classmate told me, "You can't be a doctor when you grow up, because you're a Christian Scientist," did it dawn on me just how much I didn't understand it. Even though I didn't connect with it, I was never upset with my mom for sending me. I was more than happy to spend time with my GrandMary, and my mom hadn't yet learned that morality is not a product of religious teachings but a by-product of the physiology and evolution of the human brain.

In middle school, my parents did allow me the social outlet of attending a Baptist spring break church camp lest I remain bored out of my gourd at home, an only child whose neighborhood friends were all at the camp. There, where no bikinis were allowed, I was shamed for my one-piece swimsuit not being modest enough, and I was fire and brimstone lecture-scared in an emergency group gathering moments after my Beastie Boys cassette tape was discovered. "Contraband with the devil's drum beats," they called it. (Phew, they never learned about my "vodka in the plastic hairspray bottle" trick.) Somehow, however, I did get caught up in the *come on down to be saved* moment because my underdeveloped pubescent brain thought, "What if this really *is it*?! And I wanted to fit in with the cool kids, who were duped into doing it too. After that camp, I even went as far as attending the church to get baptized all on my own; my parents did not come to watch, which was fine by my friends' parents, who reassured me that they would be there for me that day and every day thereafter.

Not long into my newly saved life, I started catching on to their hypocrisy and bigotry. Yeah, sure, my GrandMary was faithful to a nutty set of beliefs and practices, but I couldn't tolerate for a second those Baptist women shit-talking her for it. And one of the dads, a closeted drunk, lost my respect when he made the mistake of preach-advising me about being a girl who should "be careful not to march to the beat of your own drummer, cuz, honey, it's like you're marching to the beat of your own damn band." I eventually laughed at them in my rearview mirror when they held a special prayer circle to call upon the Lord to restore a Merry Christmas for a family whose van was robbed of bags of Christmas gifts from the mall parking lot. And again when the preacher's daughter got caught in a vicious act of road skull when her boyfriend rear-ended the car in front of them. I left their toxic cesspool of worldly judgment behind.

My partner Ernesto's parents also did not attend church. Neither did any of his grandparents. Though he and his sister did attend some born-again Christian type camps while visiting family in South Florida, probably for the horseback riding opportunity the camps offered. He remembers his sister was a skeptic even at such a young age. He also remembers going with the flow like I had and becoming born-again while there.

By the time middle school came, he started realizing he had friends who went to church regularly and asked his dad if he could go too, to which his dad replied something along the lines of "If you want to attend a service, you are welcome to, but I'll not be going with you." Ernesto went two or three times with his friends to a Baptist church but didn't think anything of it. Throughout his sister's childhood cancer battle, his family remained steadfast agnostics and atheists, and she beat the odds that were stacked against her.

Ernesto says he had a big religious awakening in the tenth grade. During the summer before tenth grade, he had been in Puerto Rico and attended a Catholic mass with his mom's then partner's parents. He thought it was cool for its rituals, and the *abuelita* wanted him to learn something about religion, so he told her that he'd try to learn about Catholicism. He went through the first communion and became a confirmed Catholic. His mom did some of the classes with him, but at the point where they had to profess belief in the doctrine of transubstantiation, she was out. He went through with it, eating the bread body and drinking the wine blood, but didn't stick around.

In college, Ernesto had started studying various political movements and found his emerging radical politics crossing paths with the Catholic Worker Movement and liberation theology. Working-class revolutions and siding with poor people captured his attention, so for a short-lived period of time he started attending mass again. Ultimately, he stuck with the politics and dropped the church, but it was during the aftermath of 9/11 that he finally became radical in his disbelief. Through reading, study, and critical reflection, Ernesto became an out and proud atheist and has never looked back.

In addition to not having religious tradition to uphold for our families of origin, we never felt a responsibility to make religion part of our kids' education, other than to tell them that religion is something ingrained in cultures all over the world that is important to a lot of people. Because of our own upbringings, we did not think they would be disadvantaged by not being brought up with any particular faith tradition. On the contrary, we thought they'd be better off not being compelled to adopt any faith tradition, as some religious beliefs and practices are psychologically damaging, for example, authoritarianism, separatism, and fear. We thought they'd be better off being brought up with critical thinking skills in a literacy-rich environment, and, in hindsight, some of the values that Dan Arel advocates in *Parenting without God*—secularism, separation of church and state (freedom of religion vs. freedom from religion), and a healthy trust in science.

Having just a foundational understanding of what neuroscientists have discovered over the last fifty years about human brain development reinforced our approach to parenting freethinking children. Until around seven years old, children are more susceptible to religious indoctrination, because they lack the requisite cognitive development that yields abstract reasoning. Therefore, indoctrinating young children with religion is exploitive. At around eight years old, however, children can start to see the idea of God as weird fantasy fiction, akin to continued belief in Santa or the tooth fairy. This stage of reasoning ability continues until the early teen years when children's brains become capable of more abstract thinking. Considering these developmental stages, children growing up without God have the freedom to imagine, explore, question, and ultimately decide for themselves what they believe or do not believe.

We also did not want to reinforce or give strength to religious dogma's sidekicks, aka religious baggage, all of which are human inventions of power play, excellent for keeping the masses pacified instead of empowered to question authority and systems of oppression. We saw this baggage as an interference to raising freethinking children who are encouraged to make critically thought-out decisions. This particular baggage includes but is not limited to the keeping of religious rules and doctrinal requirements, sexism and misogyny found in religious texts, homophobia, guilt, judgment, and hypocrisy, all of which are misguided burdens instead of tools that aid freedom. Plus, the belief that God is actually an angry, vengeful Big Brother is rather creepy and anxiety-inducing, as is the concept of eternal punishment and torture in Hell, the latter of which runs counter to one of the ideas we'd integrated as essential to raising freethinking children—parenting without rewards or punishments.

Not until our older child Emma-Joy hit kindergarten did being raised God-free even come up in casual conversation with her. One evening, while she was taking her before bedtime bath, I overheard her reciting the Pledge of Allegiance. I leaned my head in to ask, "What's that you're saying?" She matter-of-factly answered, "Oh, it's some stupid prayer thing we have to say at school, and I don't even believe in God." "Okay, good," I thought to myself, "she's oblivious to both religious and nationalistic indoctrination just like I was when I was a kid." A few years later, in second grade, she found herself at odds with a classmate who told her, "You're going to Hell, because you don't believe in God." While Ernesto and I were impressed by how her teacher handled the situation, Emma-Joy remained upset about that classmate's rudeness not about the "Hell" part. (Nice morals you got there, indoctrinated kid!) The truth is that if it hadn't been an argument about God, it would have been an argument about an Uglydoll or a jump rope trick. In other words, kids, generally speaking, are good at finding things to pick at each other over, not just an outlying kid's religion-free upbringing.

Our younger child has had similar experiences. Up until they started public school, their Godlessness wasn't an issue. And similar to Emma-Joy's experience, when Maya-Rae asked about a classmate's crucifix necklace, they were questioned in return, "Do you believe in Jesus?" When Maya-Rae replied that they didn't, they were informed by their sweet, baby Jesus-loving peers, "Ooooooohhhh, you're going down there," while sassily pointing down at the playground's wood chips, invoking the mythical hellscape they'd been threatened with at home and church. Another time, after dying their hair a magenta color to be in character (Strawberry Shortcake) for Favorite Book Character Day at school, a classmate complained, "Maya-Rae reminds me of the devil," and they were called down to the counselor to talk about it. They say they only remember nodding and saying "okay" a bunch because they didn't understand what the counselor was talking about or why they were even there.

Emma-Joy, now a young adult, says that now that she is older, she appreciates being raised without religion but still enjoyed learning about religions from around the world without that information being withheld from her whenever she had questions. She is a perfect example of a person who was raised without religion without being forced to be an atheist. Replacing teaching dogma with teaching critical thinking skills does that, even when tragedy struck and she did not have a god to fall back on.

Raising "unaffiliated" children is not about indoctrinating them to be secularists or atheists. Rather, it is about giving them—dogma-free, moral, ethical, and intelligent human beings—the tools to decide for themselves. And herein lies the most important struggle—attempting to challenge our own kids' lazy adoption of our atheism. Most kids naturally mimic what they hear from their parents, so we want to cultivate skepticism instead of praising their adoption of the position we have come to through our own deliberation, reading, and studies; in contrast to faith, atheism is a position that one arrives at after careful deliberation, coming to realize that God's existence is 99.99 percent improbable. In *Parenting without God*, Dan Arel also understands that this careful deliberation is not fostered through atheistic force-feeding, but rather through sensible parenting that fosters questioning, logic, and tolerance.

Introduction

Being a parent was never something I thought would be part of my life. However, the day my wife told me she was pregnant with our first child, I could not imagine anything else.

When she told me, we had a long discussion about what we wanted to do, but it seemed from the start we already knew. We wanted to have this child, and even though it would forever change our lives, we were ready, and we were willing.

We are a pro-choice family. Every single woman on this planet has a choice about her body and her pregnancy, but, for us, the choice was immediate, and we knew what we wanted to do. I will never forget how long those first eight weeks before we told anyone were, though I told my parents the very next day.

Everyone tells you how awesome parenting is: watching a child learn and grow, those first steps, first words, when they want to hug and kiss you, and when they tell you they love you. Everyone's right. It is awesome, but they forget to tell you what else comes with parenting: constant fear!

I live a life that seems to be engulfed in fear now. Luckily this isn't the main emotion I feel. I do not spend all my time worrying and missing out on all of the amazing things in life, but the fear is always there. Is the car seat installed correctly? Is this daycare the right daycare? Is this babysitter suited for the job? Will he be able to go to a good school and get a good education? What are the teachers going to teach him, and will they teach him historical facts or simply paint America in a perfect light? Will his school teach him evolution, or will they not even mention it, like my high school in Rochester, New Hampshire?

I fear the type of country in which he will grow up, and, as I watch it slip further and further into theocracy, I think that I need to remove him from the U.S. As I watch the news every day, I fear that the country is headed in a direction I don't want him to have to experience. Public schools are constantly under attack; the Christian right wants nothing more than to enact school voucher systems that will destroy public schools and funnel tax dollars to private religious schools. I fear, as I see laws progress toward equality, that one major election could change all of that. Laws like the Defense of Marriage Act (DOMA) could be reinstated, sending us back to the dark ages when only some marriages were recognized by the federal government.

That's right, I fear everything from who is watching him and what he eats to a future still a few decades away. However, I cannot call these fears unjustified. I am a loud and outspoken atheist. I believe in secular values, and I trust science. I believe in a good, strong education, and I will not let certain religious fundamentalists take that away from my son. This is why I am a secular-humanist parent. Not because I read books about parenting and decided I would do attachment—secular—parenting, but because no matter what style of parenting my wife and I chose, we would be secular parents.

My children are going to grow up in a house where the gods of all religions are a myth. They will not be told of everlasting life or eternal punishment. They will not get their moral values from a book that condones slavery, incest, and rape. And because of this, because of the choices we have made in our lives that led us to the realization that gods are nothing more than man-made creations, our children are going to be outcasts in society and in their school. Because of that, I will have to arm them with the tools to combat the criticism that will be thrown their way, and I have a duty to teach them critical thinking so that they may come to their own conclusions about life.

Being a parent is a lot of work. It is an overwhelming task with great personal rewards, and regardless of whether you are Christian, Muslim, or atheist, as a parent, you face an amazing number of challenges. I am from the United States, a predominantly Christian nation, and choosing to raise my children away from any church comes with a significant level of controversy, and that inspired me to write this book.

When I began blogging, I knew I wanted to write about the challenges of secular parenting. How do you raise a child in an atheist household and not force the child to be an atheist? Isn't that exactly what we stand against in religious households? How do you deal with tragedy when you do not have a god to fall back on? How exactly do you deal with schools and education? What do you do about bullies at school and teachers who do not recognize that not all their students subscribe to the same religious myths about holidays or about good and evil?

These problems and many more are unique to secular parenting. Many parenting problems may be universal, but the answers may be drastically different if you don't think all life is in God's hands. So I decided it was time to write a book about secular parenting. I approached my wife and she said, "Why? It's so easy!" I sat with that for a few minutes and realized it wasn't. Parenting alone is very hard; rewarding, yes, but hard. How are we going to address issues of religion with our son? How is he going to explain to his friends that he lives in a house that does not believe in the god in whom they believe, and how is he going to respond to threats of Hell?

I think parenting is less a set of rules and more a set of shared ideas. I believe that sharing my ideas may spark your own that fit your family's unique situations. So instead of reading each page as if these were rules, read each page for inspiration and for ideas about what you can do.

In each chapter I will address key issues among those that other parents have asked about most frequently. I hope this book helps start a discussion around the world and brings atheist and secular parents together to form a strong community and help each other raise their children in a world that to all appearances is run by religious believers.

Issues will range from my reflections on how I would handle various situations through my thoughts on the current state of affairs in the U.S., from gender equality, politics, science, and education to how to explain to your child that places exist where people gather together to talk to imaginary gods.

Throughout a child's life they will deal with others telling them about Hell and other religious beliefs, and, as parents, the best thing we can do is to prepare our children with the knowledge and tools to handle the beliefs of others around them.

Many atheist parents know the fear of teaching their children to be atheist. Most believe atheism is a place you should find on your own; critical thinking, knowledge, logic, and other means of rational thought lead people to reject the idea of man-made gods and consider themselves atheists. Atheism is not something atheist parents wish to indoctrinate into their children.

How, though, do you instill these values as an atheist parent without force-feeding your children? This is why I wrote this book. Parents must teach their kids to question assumptions and social norms, showing them how to think critically and be skeptical of claims that sound too good to be true.

Instill logic, and show them how to apply it to life's problems, as well as to the claims made by those around them. Teach them about as many religious beliefs as possible and also about disbelief. Explain why Christians believe in Jesus and God, Muslims in their prophet Muhammad and Allah. Teach them about Buddhism and Hinduism. Explain how different parts of the world and different types of religion think about the texts differently. Explain creation myths but at the same time impart scientific truths.

By telling your child about religious beliefs, stories, and myths, you will expose them to the world in which we live and allow them to ask questions and reflect on what they have learned. These tools will allow them to make informed and educated decisions about what they choose to believe.

Let them explore these beliefs, even if they do not align with your own. This does mean you need to let them foster hateful beliefs. If you see that their beliefs are leading to bigotry and intolerance, you should intervene, as any good parent would. But allow your child to read and learn about beliefs and religions they may find interesting. Be there to answer questions and nurture their curiosity.

You must also teach them about science and the scientific method. You do not have to be a scientist, or even understand all of the theories and laws that make up our universe, to show them how to trust and also question science. Show them science versus pseudoscience, how to tell the difference and why people make pseudoscientific claims. Teach them about the beauty of evolution, the wonder of the big bang, and just how massive and undiscovered much of our universe is. The wonders of our universe are far greater than any mythological story you can conjure up from any religion.

I also hope this book can be a part of the dialogue between the millions of secular parents around the world, and that we can all come together to share our ideas and learn from each other, piece by piece, as we grow, just as our children do through our collective experience.

You don't have to agree with everything I write. You may disagree with some of my methods or political beliefs. This is okay; I only ask that you question what I write and see how it applies to your life. No two parents are the same. I cannot expect that everything that works for me will work for you, but I hope that I can light a spark. You may disagree with something I write, but maybe it will inspire you to find the method that works for you.

This book is not a manifesto or your everyday how-to. It is a collection of thoughts and ideas that I found important enough to share, ideas that I think can set our future generations down a path of equality.

You will notice that I reference the United States throughout the book. That's because that is where I live, and it has the government and society I understand best. If you live outside the U.S., bear with me. I believe many of these ideas are cross-cultural and are not bound by the borders that we have created. You may live in a better or worse environment, and it is certainly not my intention to exclude you by focusing on the U.S.

I also refer most commonly to the Christian religion. If I do not specify a religion, you can be sure I mean the Christian faith, and often the evangelical movement in the U.S., I do my best to make any other religious references specific.

Atheists inside the U.S. are often criticized for not being hard enough on other religions and only attacking Christianity. This could not be further from the truth. I believe I make it more than clear that I have no love for any religion but write from my perspective in the U.S. Judaism and Islam have very little effect on my day to day life—but the Christian right sure does.

I have no problem discussing the vile and immoral beliefs of Islam, from honor killings to female genital mutilation in some predominantly Muslim cultures. I can go on at length about certain practices in Judaism, such as mohels putting children's penises in their mouths, which is disgusting enough without the stories of the resultant spread of herpes! Yet, as much as I despise and protest against these actions, they play very little direct part in my parenting. I will obviously raise my child to oppose any action that lessens the welfare of another sentient being, but to go into all religious practices I am against that exist largely outside of my own culture would be a fruitless act that would detract from the overall purpose of this book.

I hope some of those reading this are from outside of my culture, and I hope they take my ideas and expand on them or figure out how to apply them to their particular society. Maybe you live in a predominantly Islamic country, and you picked up this book; I think the contents are very relevant to your life, although the politics may be different. My advice on being out and open may also be seen differently if your safety is threatened.

I encourage all the readers to reach out to me with their own stories and journeys and to show me areas of my own upon which they have expanded or for which they found a different and better approach. I think creating a strong secular parenting community is key. Sharing ideas and correcting each other, or at the least telling each other about our respective experiences, will help ensure that other parents don't make those same mistakes we have.

Dealing with Religion

Teaching Religion

Teaching religion to your children is no easy task, especially for an atheist. Of course, religion should be taught, because it is such a major part of our world culture regardless of what you believe. But how do you begin? On what religions do you focus? And how do you properly teach that some people actually believe in talking snakes without ridiculing those people in front of your child?

It is important to remember that these are works of fiction and should be taught as such. We do not teach Greek mythology as "maybe true." We treat it as the fiction we know it to be, and modern-day religions are really no different. Even if a deity of sorts was to be discovered, I think we can easily agree it would not be anything dreamed up by any of the world's religions.

It is easy to think that by rejecting religion wholly you are doing your kids a disservice and indoctrinating them as atheists. You're not. You are not going to teach them about Zeus, carefully not mentioning that it is mythology. This also goes for all the world's religions. If you know something is made up, call it made up. The Bible, the Quran, they are a farce. Teach them as such.

As stated before, even if a magical man appeared in the sky tomorrow proving he was the creator of all things on earth, this would not change the fact that religious books are myths. Anthropological and historical evidence prove this. So now that we have got that out of the way, let's discuss some good ways to teach religion.

I was taught one religion, my parent's religion. I was taught a little about other religions, mostly other forms of Christianity and a little bit about Judaism. This is not the best way to teach a child about religion, and I would not recommend it.

Teach all the major religions, Catholicism and other forms of Christianity, Islam, Judaism, and you can work in the extras like Mormonism and Scientology later. Don't overwhelm your children, start from simple beginnings. Much of the Torah and the Old Testament are the same, so you can easily start there and cover Christianity and Judaism, providing information a bit at a time. Maybe a weekly chat. It doesn't have to be overly formal or school-like. Use examples from the news and the outside world to explain why things are happening and why or how people's beliefs play into these events.

This is also a good time to talk about creation myths that have been debunked through scientific evidence. Each religion and all cultures have their own creation story. It is important that children know this and understand that they are in fact myths. Understanding them and how they were debunked is a great tool for understanding how science works. Teaching religion and teaching science will often go hand in hand, from creationism, contrasting what we actually know from the DNA record and fossils with the Adam and Eve myth, to the great flood and the archaeological and geological evidence that has disproved a great flood of this biblical proportion.

How religion came to be and why it still exists is also an interesting discussion. If these stories are fake, why are they still around? Shouldn't we have grown out of them, or should they not have died off like previous religions?

I think the short answer here is yes, and eventually religions like Islam and Christianity will die off. If you really think about it, they are not that old in comparison to human history. Yes, they are old, much older than previous religions were when they died off, but religion is now more ingrained in our culture than ever before. This makes it much harder for it to just die off naturally, although we can see that it is doing so, as each year fewer and fewer people embrace a religious affiliation. The "nones" (people who check "none" on a census form next to religion) comprise the fastest growing "religion" in the U.S. That is inspiring.

Ancient cultures could not explain natural occurrences the way we can today. They did not have science or the scientific method. The sun rising and setting was beyond their comprehension. Earthquakes, storms, and all sorts of natural disasters or wonders confused them, so they made up stories to explain what was happening.

We can still see this today, for example, when less-than-honest religious leaders blame natural disasters in the U.S. on things like same-sex marriage or abortion. For some reason, they believe that when their god doesn't like same-sex marriage, the best way to tell us is to kill hundreds of people in a tornado in the Bible Belt. Nothing gets a message across like killing those who worship you!

People are scared of things they do not understand, so it makes a lot of sense that ancient people would have created good forces, such as gods, to protect them and bad forces for things they were afraid of or knew to be dangerous. What better way to prevent children from exploring dangerous areas or going into the dark than with stories of evil beings?

These ideas make sense, as does their growth. Christianity was part of a power grab. How better to control Rome than to unify everyone under one belief and one set of "holy" rules. It was never an accident that many of those rulers who learned to harness the power of religion also seemed to have a direct line to God himself. This convenient fact most certainly helps when enacting laws, given that they come directly from God.

Explaining this helps show how religious myths move and evolve from culture to culture. It enables us to understand how something untrue can so easily continue to be believed, as it develops and morphs to fit with the norms and morals of different societies.

Then there are some bigger subjects upon which to focus when discussing religion with your children. Teaching that religion exists is one thing but diving into what adherents believe and why those beliefs are harmful is another.

Many of us we were taught to not discuss religion or politics. These seem to always be taboo subjects. In more recent years, this taboo has been stripped away when it comes to politics, and it seems everywhere you go politics is being discussed, with everyone wanting to share their opinions or analysis. Yet religion has managed to position itself so that people still feel it is out of bounds.

The idea that religion is untouchable is crumbling, and we can pass this torch on to our children. Some of our children may grow up to be religious or simply indifferent to religion, not identifying with it but feeling no particular desire to speak out against it. However, they should always feel comfortable speaking about it if they wish, just as they should about all bad ideas.

Religion needs to be on the table. We have the right to critique, praise, or criticize religious actions at any time and for any reason. This starts by teaching our children about religion, its place in the world, and its history. It also starts by not promoting the idea that certain things should not be discussed.

We are at a turning point in the world, a point where more and more people are leaving religion behind. With each new generation, more children are being raised in houses that do not attend church or discuss religion, even if the parents continue to claim to believe in such gods.

This presents us with a unique opportunity to raise children who are able to think critically and question assumptions.

While it is great to think about parents not forcing a religion on children, they do them a disservice by ignoring it or just accepting it at face value. These children will not be equipped to question such ideas when they are inevitably presented with them. They are at risk for simply accepting a stated belief as fact. This is exactly what the religious leaders around the world want. We should not give this to them.

Teaching religion does not come easy, but there are many reasons we must. There are numerous beliefs intrinsic to religion that should be broken down: Heaven, Hell, sin, ideas about sex, faith, and the physical and mental abuse that comes along with some of the fundamental (and sometimes not so fundamental) beliefs of various religions.

We are going to explore these different aspects of religion and break them down to better understand them. It is that understanding that we, in turn, will pass on to our children, which will gradually change the course of religious domination, not only in the U.S. but around the world.

My goal of changing how the world thinks about religion is not to make people stop believing in a god or gods. I care little about what people privately believe. However, I care deeply about what they do with those beliefs. If their religious beliefs teach intolerance and hatred, are used to support war, genocide, female genital mutilation, honor killings, or laws that protect or honor such rituals or beliefs, then we have a problem, and I will stand up against every such instance and fight it with every means available to me.

This is a battle that can be won with education. No blood need be shed to rid the world of such beliefs. They will fall victim to reason, logic, and evidence. These beliefs have a terrible weakness, and that weakness is the power of the human mind when used to its full potential.

It will not be a bullet or a sword that kills religion, or even kills God; it will be the rational mind. These poisonous ideas only exist in the minds of those who hold them to be true. By raising generations of critical thinkers, we begin to weaken this virus that infects the minds of many people. Reason can be looked at like a vaccine. With reason, you teach a child to block and combat such ideas and introduce them to different ways of thinking and processing information.

This is a good time to note something that is very common in the atheist community: the idea that religion is a mental illness. It is not, and claiming it is insults those who suffer from real mental illnesses. It also suggests that we could cure someone of religion with medicine. We cannot and will not. Religion is not a disease in the medical sense. It is in the social sense, and just as we call faith a virus knowing full well there is no actual virus, religion and faith are ideas that exist in the mind and are cured through rational thought, reason, and logic.

Many people suffer at the hands of religion, and some may have underlying mental illnesses that allow religion to take further advantage of them, but would anyone reading this who used to be religious claim that they used to have a mental illness? I doubt it. Most often the people who are told they have a mental illness are those who do the unthinkable or are so blinded by faith they reject obvious evidence. A parent who lets their child die or be abused in the name of religion may have their own set of mental issues, but it isn't religion. Religion was the driving force that preyed on those mental issues and guided their ideas about how to care for their children, but not every time. Many parents who have let their children die of curable diseases in the name of Christian Science and faith-based healing have not suffered from known mental illness, but their ability to reason had been destroyed by religious brainwashing and indoctrination. They don't necessarily suffer from a mental problem, but they suffer from a lack of reason and are unable to tell fact from fiction, because they were raised in a way that robbed them of that ability, usually at a young age. I raise this because I do not want people teaching their children that those who believe religious claims have a mental illness. I would prefer that they believe religion is what it is: a socially constructed belief system that can lead people to do very terrible things. It is a social construct that can and should be destroyed, but it is not an illness.

When logic, rationality, critical thinking, skepticism, or any other form of questioning is applied to religion, it begins to fall apart at the base. Religion will not tumble if we only aim for the top. We must go after its groundwork. We must start in the very basement of these ideas. With each brick we remove, the foundation becomes more unstable. If we can destroy the foundation, the rest will crumble under its own weight. This is where victory is won. This is how we begin to change the world.

Just as Rome was not built in a day, religion will not fall overnight. Our children will be lucky if they are the ones to witness its demise, but the deconstruction starts now.

Religion is easy to discard. It offers nothing that humanity does not already have, and anything good that comes from religion is pure coincidence. The Bible offers zero moral guidance that did not exist before religion and that could not exist after. So while I respect the rights of individuals to have any beliefs they please, I see no reason to offer these beliefs any respect and absolutely no reason to allow them a place in public policy.

When politicians allow their religious beliefs to dictate any form of public policy, there is a guarantee it will result in the oppression of and discrimination against those outside of their belief system. This is clearly against everything the Founding Fathers had in mind when they drafted the U.S. Constitution and set forth to create a secular country.

The world we are trying to create for our children has no room for an American theocracy, and it will only be when more parents stand up and say enough is enough, do their best to educate our children on religion and its harm, and raise them to know it is okay to question and criticize these beliefs without fear that we will set a course for a future that sees the religious reign of terror eradicated. One day people will look back and tell stories of their ancestors who believed in sky gods and took their moral guidance from a book as silly as the Bible.

The LGBTQ communities, minority communities, atheists, humanists, and anyone else who stands outside the religious ideas about what is normal will only be able to claim a victory when our country finally gets off its hands and rebuilds the wall that separates church and state.

Religion and religious belief do not need to be wiped off the planet for this to be achieved, but they do have to be put in their place. That place is inside churches, synagogues, temples, and other places of worship, including your own home, but not in the daily lives of citizens who have chosen to have nothing to do with it.

Religion should be kept far away from our public schools. Many make the argument that it belongs in a theology class, but theology should be a college elective not a subject taught to young impressionable students going through the grade school system. If religion is brought up, it should only be in a historical context. A history class is the perfect place to discuss the explosion of Christianity and the Middle Ages, the crusades, and acts such as 9/11 that were based in religion, because ignoring the religious influence would hurt the student's education.

Prayer has not left our schools. The claim that it has is an outright dishonest statement by the Christian right, which attempts to blame violence, such as school shootings, on the lack of religion in our schools. The truth is that only prayer led by a teacher or staff member has been removed from schools. Students are more than welcome to pray on their own or in groups, but the school's staff cannot lead it. It is as simple as that.

When politicians are debating a bill in Congress, no longer should they be yelling about what the Bible says or their own beliefs. They should only be debating about what is good for the American people. Enough majoritarianism; it is time to bring in an age of egalitarianism.

The Declaration of Independence states all men are created equal, and it is about time we finally realize that we are all equal. If we cannot do this, our country cannot last, and if we do not do this, ours will be a country in which we do not want to raise our children.

It is not the genitals you have, the color of your skin, the income level of you or your family, and most certainly not which mythical being you worship or do not worship that grant you any rights or privileges in this country or any-where else in the world. What matters is how you conduct yourself, how you treat others, and the decisions you make. If you murder someone, you lose privileges. Not because you are poor, black, or Latino, but simply because you broke a law and acted in a way that hurt someone else's well-being and ended their life without consent. No amount of money should allow you to pay your way out of being punished for crimes. Issues like poverty need to be resolved to help keep people out of the dire situations that spawn desperation and the resultant crime.

All too often, we blame the victim of our social inequal-ity. The time has come to put an end to this way of thinking. Religion has taught us that some people are worth more than others. This is a reprehensible message that should be paved over with a new, secular message of a true egalitarian society that puts moral weight on issues that matter and removes the faux moral arguments from things such as marriage and consensual adult sex.

Religious influence on society can and will be stopped. You and I are the people to do it, and we continue the work through our children. Intolerance will not be accepted, inequality will be squashed, and we will look upon every man, woman, and child not as a commodity but as a sentient being deserving of the utmost respect.

Faith-Based Healing

Christian Scientists (as they are called for some very strange reason) rely on faith for just about everything. No matter how severe your illness or injury, they rely on prayer for healing. They even have "doctors" who will pay you a house visit and pray for you. This often results in death or long-term disabilities.

Many states in the U.S. allow parents to make the decision to bypass modern medicine and rely on faith-based healing for their children. As discussed in Sean Faircloth's book *Attack of the Theocrats,* this has devastating consequences.[1] Children with tumors the size of softballs go untreated until, in agonizing pain, they succumb to the disease and die.

While in the U.S. we proudly boast that we have religious freedom, laws need to be implemented to protect children from their parents' faith-based decisions. The mind of a child cannot rationalize these decisions properly, and the child should not be put in known risk. Treatment for curable illnesses should be administered to anyone under the age of eighteen regardless of their parent's irrational beliefs.

All fifty states should outlaw faith-based healing practices for anyone under the age of eighteen. If a child is sick, they should be given the best possible care modern medicine can offer, regardless of the wishes of the parents. Their failed

---

1   Sean Faircloth, *Attack of the Theocrats: How the Religious Right Harms Us All—and What We Can Do About It* (Charlottesville, VA: Pitchstone Publishing, 2012).

epistemologies should not result in the death or suffering of any child.

My personal friend Liz Heywood is an outspoken activist against faith-based healing. Liz grew up in a Christian Science home in Massachusetts. She fell off her horse one day and broke her leg severely. Rather than seek medical attention, her parents relied on prayer. In later adulthood, Liz had to have her leg amputated because the damage done from the injury going untreated was irreversible.

The pain and agony Liz and countless others in this world are forced to endure because of their parents' misguided decisions can and should be stopped. Lives of innocent children are lost because of pure ignorance. A parent truly believes prayer will heal their child of an illness, and when the child's life is lost, they are told it was all a part of God's plan.

Faith spreads like a virus. We must inoculate our children early and teach them the importance of questioning people's beliefs and claims, especially when they are faith-based beliefs. Any belief that is not based in evidence is irrational and should be questioned until either evidence is provided or the belief is discarded.

The problem with faith is that if you make decisions based on pretending to know things you don't know, you run the risk of making very risky decisions. In faith-based healing, we have what would be seemingly good people making very bad, life-threatening decisions because of a reliance on a belief system that is not based on sound knowledge or understanding. They believe God will heal the sick or wounded through prayer alone. However, the evidence stands against what they claim to know, and yet they willfully ignore this evidence, because it contradicts their belief system. God will not heal anyone, and prayer is, for all intents and purposes, useless.

Pretending to know something like this means you will not second-guess your decisions, because you really do believe the facts are on your side. This is why faith is a failed epistemology. It is not a sufficient way of knowing things, which is what makes teaching our children about more efficient ways of discovering facts or truth so important.

Believing you know something and not questioning it is just dangerous and unacceptable, so we should use the Socratic method, the scientific method, and be skeptical about claims made by others to root out what is true and what is not.

Going to Church

One day your child will ask you about church. What exactly do you say? How do you explain that it's a place where deluded people talk to and worship an imaginary being? Do you flat-out insult the idea? What if their friends are discussing church with them? Surely insulting church can't be the right way to discuss it, but it's going to come up, and we must address it.

Church is a tricky situation. Your child is going to meet kids through school, sports, and other activities who go to church, and they will hear, "Come with me," as churches love youth groups and outings as a way to suck children into religion as young as possible. So what can we do? How do you avoid being the mean parent who doesn't let your child have fun with their friends but at the same time keeps them away from dangerous religious indoctrination?

I am sorry to say there is no easy answer here. In all honesty, until you believe your child is old enough to understand the concepts being taught to them, has the ability to think about them critically, and has the strength to stand up to things that they may not agree with (such as talking negatively about gay rights, women's rights, etc.), I would not let your child attend these events. I went to these events as a child. Looking back, I know now they are nothing but brainwashing seminars where a cool and hip pastor takes the stand to make Christianity more appealing to a young, impressionable crowd. At the time, however, I was taken in and believed every word, leading to years of further religious indoctrination.

Now let's not forget about another major church problem: our parents. Many atheists grew up religious and still have religious parents who will want to bring their child to church. For me, this is a huge "NO!" Same rules as above apply; if your child is the right age to think critically and wants to go, then let them. You cannot shield them forever, but you need to keep in mind that as children and young teenagers, they will see the minister as an authority figure. This is dangerous, because we have taught our children that authority figures, such as teachers and parents, are to be listened to, and instructions from them should be followed. They will in most cases see a minister in this light, especially a very charismatic one.

Telling your parents that your child cannot attend church with them may not be easy, but as a parent, you must protect your child as best you can. I am very much against shielding children from religion, but introduction to it should be on your terms not anyone else's, and certainly not the religion's own terms. Catholics, for example, are less likely to be critical of their religion, Evangelicals of theirs, and so on.

This same advice applies to parents of your children's' friends. Think about Saturday night sleepovers. Will the parents want to bring your child to their church on Sunday morning? I know that when I was growing up, some of my friends' parents did, and I cannot remember a time they asked my parents first. They just did it. In fact, I can only remember one time my parents knew I was asked and refused to let me go, because they didn't approve of the brand of Christianity. I was Pentecostal, the other family was Episcopalian. I guess in the Christian world that is Bloods versus Crips.

I would advise a secular or atheist parent to be very diligent about your child's activities. Know with whom they are hanging out and who their parents are. Will their friend's parents grill your child about religion? Again, I know from personal experience this happens. Especially when a family views religion as a core part of their household, they will bring this up the second they can.

If you are an outspoken activist atheist you are probably already well aware that your actions will affect your child's life. This is not necessarily bad, but it means you will need to give extra attention to how your child reacts to religious questions from others. How do they answer a barrage of questions? What do they do if they happen to be asked to leave? And, most important, explain to them they may lose some friends whose parents do not want their child playing with a kid who has parents "like us."

That's worst case. I hope we are finally starting to live in a society that's more accepting, and fewer parents would hold a child accountable for their parents' beliefs. After all, there is no atheist, Christian, or Muslim child. There are only children of atheist, Christian, or Muslim parents. We are quick to forget this fact, because religion means that from the moment of birth, you share your parent's religion. Children can have "Catholic parents," but until a child is old enough to make decisions on their own they truly have no religion.

It's easy to make children your billboard. I always wanted to put my son in a Darwin tee shirt, because I knew how much it would upset people, but is my son a Darwinist? No, he doesn't even understand who Darwin was. He will, so help me, but right now he does not. Now, a Nirvana or Smiths tee shirt, that's fair game.

I jokingly comment often about atheist children, because, in a way, they all are; if you know nothing of belief, nothing of a deity, then you do not automatically start believing. Belief in a god must be learned. You do not come to these conclusions on your own. Atheism, however, I see as a natural state. If no one tells you of such things, then you won't start believing them. We don't have words for people who don't believe in astrology or unicorns. So why a word for people who don't believe in an illogical concept such as god?

As an atheist or secular parent, you are something of a role model, not only for your kids but also for atheism in general. This may sound like a role you didn't ask to play, and in a way it is, however, you are a trailblazer setting the example for other parents. It is widely believed that good only comes from religion, and that one can only be good if one believes in God. It's unthinkable to many people that those who reject the idea of God could possibly have morals.

This is where humanism comes in: "good without a god." Meet your child's friend's parents well before any religious conversation arises. Show them you are a good person, a great parent, and trustworthy, then if the time comes when they discover you are not a believer, they may have a whole new concept of what that means or, at the very least, the courage to discuss it with you if it concerns them. However, whatever concerns they have may pale in comparison to the discussion you may need to have with them about what is appropriate to discuss with your own child. This will also mean being diligent in asking your child what was discussed at dinner at their friend's house and what movies they watched at the sleepover.

This may seem like hovering and excessive worrying, and I am not saying you need to freak out over everything that comes up, but this will allow you to know where your child is at and what, if anything, you need to discuss with them about what other people believe and why you personally do not believe it. This comes back to the idea that we need to make sure our children understand they can ask us anything. If someone in the schoolyard tells them about religion, and it scares or concerns them, they should know they can talk to you at any time about it. Threats of Hell are a scary thing. The religious know this, and that's why they are so quick to bring this up with children. They know they can get a child to run to God out of fear alone. They will tell your child that their parents, as atheists, will burn in Hell forever if they don't repent. Religion thrives on using death to control its followers, and death is a subject with which, as parents, we will be forced to deal. Religious parents are quick to fall back on their faith. Answering death questions is easy when you can say that grandma or grandpa are waiting in Heaven.

Is Religion Child Abuse?

It seems almost cliché to call religion child abuse. What author or writer looking to be the next Richard Dawkins hasn't used this method? Dawkins, of course, first brought this up in his best seller *The God Delusion*, which discussed the effects on a child of teaching them about Hell, etc.[1]

I think most atheists and nonbelievers agree that religion has a negative effect on a child, though not all would go so far as to call it child abuse. More probably should, though, and one reason they don't is the many crimes against children in the name of religion seem to get a media pass, with only those who pay close attention to international news sources getting these stories.

One could write an entire book on the laws that allow religious institutions to get away with murder, or, at the very least, negligent homicide, and in fact Sean Faircloth did just that. In Faircloth's book, *Attack of the Theocrats,* he addresses states that allow religious childcare facilities to go uninspected.[2] Some of those facilities have been responsible for the deaths of children who were neglected or forgotten inside of hot vans on summer afternoons, because the facility was understaffed, under-trained, and not required to meet certain training and safety guidelines. Accidents happen, of course, but rules and regulations are put into

1 Richard Dawkins, *The God Delusion* (Boston: Mariner Books, 2008).
2 Sean Faircloth, *Attack of the Theocrats: How the Religious Right Harms Us All—and What We Can Do About It* (Charlottesville, VA: Pitchstone Publishing, 2012).

place to help minimize the chance of such accidents. Yet in states like Alabama, if you claim your childcare facility is affiliated to a religion, none of those rules and regulations apply.

I will not attempt here to recreate Faircloth's book, but I do highly recommend everyone read it. What I do want to look at, though, are some of the fundamental ways religion is child abuse, from mental abuse, teaching kids about ever-lasting punishment of Hell and the delusion of everlasting happiness and a better world after this in Heaven, to reli-giously condoned physical abuse that has resulted in the deaths of many children.

To Train Up a Child was written by Michael and Debi Pearl.[3] The Pearls own a ministry called No Greater Joy Ministries. According to the *New York Times*, the ministry brings in about 1.7 million dollars a year.[4]

Now what you find in the book on "training up" your child is mostly standard love and the demonstration of affec-tion and nurturing, but this book also fully condones and recommends physical abuse. They take a basic page from the spanking handbook by saying never strike your child in anger. However, anyone who is striking a child must harbor some level of anger. Given that spanking is rather common in the United States, this has become somewhat of a mantra for those who still practice this barbaric parenting form.

What makes this book so very different is not that it con-dones spanking, but that it condones what they call "switch-ing." Switching is described in the *New York Times*: "They

3   Michael Pearl and Debi Pearl, *To Train Up a Child: Child Training for the 21st Century* (Pleasantville, TN: No Greater Joy Ministries, 2015).

4   Erik Eckholm, "Preaching Virtue of Spanking, Even as Deaths Fuel Debate," *New York Times*, November 16, 2011, accessed June 16, 2019, http://www.nytimes.com/2011/11/07/us/deaths-put-focus-on-pastors-advocacy-of-spanking.html?_r=2&adxnnl=1&adxnnlx=1384 001324-E0/LrtDjPtqV8IOmJs5bBQ&pagewanted=all&.

teach parents to use light taps to train infants not to roll off a blanket. For older children, parents are told to respond to defiance by hitting hard enough to sting with a willow switch, a belt, a wooden spoon or the tube."

Mr. Pearl describes child rearing as a zero-sum test of wills. If a verbal warning does not work, he said, "You have the seeds of self-destruction."

If you grew up in a Christian household as I did, you may not be too shocked by some of this. I was no stranger to a wooden spoon against my backside if I defied my parent's wishes. I have seen the belt come out of the loops, and I went to an elementary school that used a wooden paddle as a form of discipline.

So what makes the Pearl's method so much different? It is the level at which this abuse is inflicted.

Hana Williams was a thirteen-year-old girl from Ethiopia. She was adopted by Larry and Carri Williams and was starved, beaten, and left outside in the freezing cold until finally hypothermia took this young girl's life.

Hana's parents used corporal punishment methods of parenting found in the book *To Train Up a Child*. As reported on Examiner.com: "The couple's abusive parenting tactics mimicked instructions from the Christian parenting book. Evidence presented at trial indicated Carri Williams had repeatedly beaten Hana with a plastic tube—a device recommended in the book."[5]

To Train Up a Child advocates using a plumbing tool to beat children starting at age one. As well as beating them, the book also advocates giving children cold water baths, putting children outside in cold weather, forcing them to miss meals, all of which exemplifies the abuse investigators

---

5   "Another Couple Found Guilty of Murder for Parenting by 'To Train Up a Child,'" ATE, November 28, 2013, accessed June 16, 2019, http://www.abovetopsecret.com/forum/thread985177/pg1.

said Hana endured, and all activities encouraged in this little book that has sold millions of copies. Hana Williams was sent to the United States from her home country with nothing but the future ahead of her, and it was taken away, because her adoptive parents were religious fundamentalists who had no problem citing the famous biblical quote, "He that spareth his rod hateth his son." Hana Williams, who froze to death outside her family home, on May 12, 2011, will never be able to realize her full potential.

Hana Williams is not alone in this tragic story. There are two other confirmed deaths of children linked directly to this one book, and other child deaths in the United States have also been caused by allowing religious exemptions. Thirty-seven states bar criminal prosecution against parents who refuse to offer medical treatment to their children for religious reasons. Preventable and curable diseases are taking the lives of America's youth, because the parents are allowed to decide that their religion trumps the child's well-being, and even their child's own wishes.

The Bible is full of horrific stories of stoning, mass murder, genocide, infanticide, and countless others crimes against humanity, and many authors have gone into great detail about these stories. We live today in a society where after every mass shooting, after every violent act carried out by any young, disenfranchised youth, we quickly blame TV and violent video games. I have to wonder why we never blame the Bible for putting such violent ideas into children's minds. It is questionable whether stories in the Bible would even be allowed on network television or in PG movies, yet we find it virtuous for a child to take an interest in such texts.

Sunday schools around the world teach children the stories of Abraham being commanded to kill his son, and this is supposed to be a positive lesson. In what world is this positive? What child needs to believe their father would do anything God commanded of them, even kill them? This sort of teaching can have a lasting effect on many children, especially those whose parents use corporal punishment in the household. A dad who will beat the hell out of you cannot seem too far from being willing to sacrifice you.

This sort of mental torment should not be tolerated. No child should fear his or her parents. Many parents instill this fear as a teaching mechanism, and I have known many people growing up whose fathers terrified them. Those children were lucky to grow up as normal functioning members of society, and I have personally seen the damage a childhood like that can do a young child, as it led to an early and tragic death of a close friend of mine. Turning to alcohol or drugs is an easy way for these kids to cope with the problems at home.

To be fair, terrible parents exist regardless of religion. Ridding the world of all religion would not solve the problem of people who simply should not be parents having kids, but when you add certain religious teachings and practices, you run the risk of putting dangerous tools and justifications into the hands of already bad parents. You also run the risk of turning well-intentioned good parents bad, because they believe the acts they are carrying out are justified in the eyes of their god and will unquestionably follow these teachings.

A major part of this problem is that the parents believe they are doing the right thing. They are not like a parent who might slap their child and be filled with guilt later. These are parents who believe they are doing the Lord's work, and we must be aware of this when attacking the root of the problem.

When it comes to religiously based mental or physical abuse of children, the underlying issue is faith. Without faith, many of these parents would not dream of doing the dreadful things they do. However, many of them were raised in similar situations. This is the life they know, and they fear the consequences of not raising their children in this manner.

Religious abuse in many cases goes back countless generations, and this use of fear is passed down. The parents reading this know that they picked up far too many parenting techniques from their own parents, but many of us have adapted. I was spanked growing up but have decided I will not spank my child. I don't look back at being spanked and think it damaged me. I don't feel it played too strong a role in who I turned out to be, but that is only me. I cannot say that my son would have the same outcome or that others would. If your father put the fear of God in you night in and night out, I don't think it would be far-fetched to think that's the kind of parent you could turn out to be. Many have not. Many did find a way out and broke the pattern, but this is not the case for everyone.

Religion has long-term effects on people, damaging effects. While we can rest assured we are not passing off these fear-based myths to our children, we should be aware that they are out there and be able to identify them. Look for children at your child's school who may be sick and untreated, have bruises, etc. This may not reveal motives based in religion, but, regardless, this is just good citizenship. If this rabbit hole does lead down a religious path, it may be harder to address than just calling the cops and reporting some bruises. Many states protect a parent's right to hit their children and to neglect medical care.

According to a 2013 report by the National District Attorneys Association, thirty-seven states, the District of Columbia, and Guam have laws providing that parents or caretakers who fail to provide medical assistance to a child because of their religious beliefs are not criminally liable for harm to the child.[6]

6   *Religious Exemptions to Child Neglect* (Arlington, VA: National District Attorneys Association, 2015), accessed June 16, 2019, https://ndaa.org/wp-content/uploads/2-11-2015-Religious-Exemptions-to-Child-Neglect.pdf.

That means that the federal government protects parents from criminal charges in thirty-seven states. Thirty-seven! Even more states allow parents to opt out of vaccinations for religious reasons, and you can opt out of certain school classes in some states if what they teach is against certain religious beliefs. For example, California, Colorado, Massachusetts, Michigan, Minnesota, and Ohio have statutes excusing students with religious objections from studying about disease.

If a parent's religion doesn't believe in "disease," they can opt their child out so they never have to learn about it. This is how the cycle continues. These parents, their church, and religious lobbyists know these children cannot learn these truths, because it would undermine the religion's future.

The secular movement needs to lobby strongly to remove all religious exemptions from children's care. No parent should be allowed to deny medical, educational, or any other right simply because the they do not want it for their child. A child is not your property to treat as you so please. A child who is not old enough to make their own life and death decisions should be cared for with the best medical, educational, and other modern-day advancements that will allow them to lead better lives with greater well-being.

We should also be looking at national educational campaigns that discuss the importance of modern medicine. These campaigns could in many ways help young and even older adults who grew up in a sheltered environment and still believe modern medicine is bad for you—is a sin, or whatever faith-based belief keeps them from seeking proper medical attention. Campaigns could highlight the effectiveness of vaccines, cancer treatment, and the treatment of minor ailments that, left unattended, can lead to bigger issues.

Secular groups could even run national campaigns reaching out to those trapped in or abused by these religions and provide them with safe places to talk to people and possibly offer legal counsel or even safe houses. Women and children often suffer great abuse, and reaching out for help can be nearly impossible, but if we were to look for them and offer help, we could do great work.

Groups like this already exist, and I recommend you check them out. There is a great nationwide group called Recovering from Religion that helps people in many different ways, ranging from abuse to mental trauma, including dealing with the endless threats of Hell and eternal torture.

Heaven

There is a very special place; you cannot see it, and you cannot touch it. I cannot even tell you anything about it, because the only book that tells you it exists mentions nothing of what lies inside.

I can tell you that it is the happiest place you can imagine, and you will see all your loved ones and not loved ones and that neighbor who always let their dog poop on your lawn and your mother-in-law who never liked you and thought your spouse could do better, and, oh, there is Hitler too. He must have asked for forgiveness. But where is grandma?

What is this magical place? This paradise that sounds a lot less peaceful when you really think about it? This place is the life about which you should be most excited? Forget this drab boring life here on earth. If you want tickets to the after-party, you just have to believe.

Heaven is a silly idea, and yet it brings comfort to millions, or I should say billions, around the earth. Worldwide, there are countless people suffering, patiently awaiting a slow death in the hopes that the life after this one will be full of joy and happiness. I understand this. I know why people long to believe Heaven is real. This life can suck for so many people. There are all those starving kids around the world, people who are raped, those who are slaves in their countries or traded into sex slavery. These terrible lives need to mean something. They need to have something better waiting for them.

We pretend that even if we cannot help them through direct action or with financial aid, we can sit at home and pray that God finds them and saves their souls. If God does not find them, these people suffering will be sentenced to more suffering. We don't want that, so let's hope God can persuade them to worship him unquestioningly. Otherwise, things only get worse.

We pretend that a child dying of cancer will soon be with the angels, and we tell their parents that their child must have been so special that God wanted them up there beside him. We allow people to live a life of delusion, because it makes them feel better, rather than enabling them to deal with reality. These same (so-called) caring people want to seek out and tell your child they must repent or burn in Hell forever.

Until these delusional proselytizers find your child, the choice about whether or not to talk about Heaven and Hell are up to you.

When it comes to teaching your child about Heaven and Hell, I personally suggest not doing either. Do not put these ideas in their head. Psychologist Susan K. Perry says in an article titled "Don't Teach Kids about Heaven": "Anytime a group extols the extraordinary rewards of death and what comes after, you're skimming the edges of being a death cult. That's how terrorists happen, if the timing and culture align a certain way."[1]

So much emphasis is put on the joy of dying that the joy of living is forgotten. We should be living this life now not dreaming about the next one, and religion, with its focus on death, is, just as Perry says, a "death cult."

Atheists on the other hand value other things. We spend our time valuing the life we have and understanding that at death, it is over. In many cases, however, someone else has already taught your child about Heaven—another parent,

---

1   Susan Perry, "Don't Teach Kids About Heaven," Creative Atheist, October 16, 2013, accessed June 16, 2019, http://www.patheos.com/blogs/creativeatheist/2013/10/dont-teach-kids-about-heaven.

a classmate, the possibilities are endless. We all know how much the believers love to talk about the afterlife with the people they don't want to see while on earth yet with whom they can't wait to spend eternity!

In the event that your child asks you about Heaven, it should be immediately laid to rest as a myth. It builds up a false hope, skews the reality of death, and leaves the child thinking there is something better after this. It undermines the reality of the world in which we live and causes people to be less active in fixing problems. Republican politicians ignore global warming signs, either because it is not predicted in the Bible, or because they believe, as does Senator Michele Bachmann, that we are living in end times, and that they will soon be reunited with their lord and savior. With that mind-set, who would be motivated to make the world a better place?

Heaven is a crutch also used as a weapon, and the idea needs to be discarded. This starts with our children and us. One needs to look no further than radical religious fundamentalists who use Heaven as a tool to recruit young men to sacrifice their lives. Much emphasis in the U.S. media is placed on the number of virgins an Islamic martyr receives when he reaches Heaven, but it is really much deeper than that. The idea of martyrdom brings great honor to oneself and one's family, and if you truly believe a paradise awaits you and your family for doing God's work, it is easy to understand why you would be willing to sacrifice your life.

Children want to believe in Heaven. If you happened to be raised in a religious environment, you can most likely remember the great feelings that the thought of Heaven gave you or the comfort you found in it when you dealt with death for the first time. While you may find it easy to use Heaven to offer your children comfort, the real question comes down to honesty. Are you doing your children any favors by lying to them and setting an unreasonable expectation? Are you running the risk of glorifying death by making an unsubstantiated claim that there is a world greater than the one in which we currently live?

So, yes, if your child is suffering and mourning the death of someone close, and you want to make it go away, it is easy to offer the tale that they will meet again someday. But they will not, so why say it? Death can be dealt with in a much more dignified and honest way, and in the grand scheme of things, the idea of Heaven tends to open up a bigger problem—Hell.

How do you assure your child that someone went to Heaven and not Hell? What proof do you have to counter the idea that their now deceased loved one is not in paradise but is suffering in hellfire?

Simple. You dispel the whole idea. What good can come from teaching Heaven? Think really hard about it, because other than making life easier on the parent who doesn't want to explain death and continuing the delusion that life carries on after death, is there any real-life reason to keep the myth alive? Does it actually help humanity to be better? I don't think so. I do not think there is even a quantifiable percentage of the population of this world who are doing good deeds and not raping and murdering people only because they think Heaven sounds nice. Besides, the forgiveness loophole means you can do all the bad things you want, as long as you remember to say sorry in the end.

So get rid of Heaven. It is a worthless delusion that clearly does more harm than good.

And Hell? Let's look at Hell a little closer.

Hell

If teaching about Heaven is bad, teaching about Hell is downright mental child abuse. There is no way around this. You are telling a child that for bad deeds done or not worshiping the right (or any) god, they are going to burn in a lake of fire for eternity. Pure torture, unimaginable pain, and it is forever.

The myth of Hell needs to be destroyed faster than the myth of Heaven by far. Children and countless adults fear their actions will result in them spending eternity in Hell. Why? It is such a childish and illogical idea. For starters, their almighty God created an evil angel and instead of destroying him gave him his own kingdom? And let's not get started on the fact that if Satan is the one punishing the bad guys for their evil, doesn't that make Satan the good guy? If Hell is for the most evil people in the world, people who listened to or worshiped Satan, wouldn't Satan be glad to have them? It simply doesn't make sense, and even Christians and other religious followers are deciding they don't believe in Hell anymore. It seems that all the rest of their religion is true, but Hell sounds too mean, so that part is obviously just an allegory. So just like the endless rape, murder, genocide, and other atrocities of the Bible, let's go ahead and cherry-pick Hell right out of it.

Now, of course, Hell gives many people a sense of justice. Hitler got the easy way out by killing himself and never answering for his crimes, yet many take comfort in the idea that he is in Hell for eternity. For nonbelievers, that comfort does not exist. We take comfort in knowing he is not alive anymore to continue causing harm. We take comfort in learning from past mistakes and working to not repeat them. Pretending that we don't have to worry about evil actions that seem foreign to us, because we believe someone else will handle it, is exactly what leads to such atrocities in the first place. It is always someone else's responsibility.

Hell comes with a lot of guilt, unnecessary guilt at that. I know a woman named Barbara (name changed) and she has a granddaughter who seems to be rather fertile. Before the age of eighteen, Barbara's granddaughter had three kids and recently found out she was going to have another. The grandchild, Jessica (name also changed), decided a fourth kid was not feasible at the time and asked Barbara to help her get an abortion.

Barbara is a very religious woman but did what she believed was right for her grandchild and drove her to the clinic and paid for the abortion. Ever since, Barbara has been sick with guilt. How will God react? Did she just sign her way out of Heaven?

Now, abortion is a personal matter. It is right for some and wrong for others, but Jessica made her decision, and Barbara did right by her, so why should she suffer in guilt and fear? When Barbara talks about this suffering, it all revolves around her religious belief and the fear that she had done something unforgivable.

The threat that her actions could send her to Hell keeps her up at night. The thought tortures her, but it doesn't need to. Leaving faith behind and realizing the threats of Hell are no more real than Santa keeping a list of good and bad kids, she could go on with her life knowing she made the decision based on the situation at hand, and that she did the best she could.

The idea of Hell is so stressful to some that support groups exist around the world for those dealing with that trauma. It's a very scary thing to believe in and to fear that one wrong move can send you there for eternity. So while retributive justice in Hell may sound great when thinking about all of the horrible people on this planet, it would also mean that good people who worshipped wrong or committed any number of religious "sins" would be forced to suffer an eternity of suffering as well.

Hell also seems to be used to justify many actions here on earth. We live in a time when the United States is one of the rare industrialized countries that has an unhealthy obsession with putting inmates to death. Since 1976, the state of Texas has put 506 inmates to death.[1] This is a number they often brag about. They love to send their criminals straight to Hell. Except, of course, they don't.

There are countless reasons to oppose the death penalty: social injustice, racial injustice, human rights, a flawed legal system—I could go on and on. However, I struggle with two major factors in this debate. First, it is the easy way out. You commit a horrible crime, and then you are put to sleep. Problem solved. You don't have to think about what you have done, and you do not have to answer to those families whose lives you destroyed. Instead, you close your eyes, go to sleep, and never know anything of it.

Second, and a much deeper and more philosophical issue, is the question of free will. If free will is nothing more than an illusion, as science suggests, then one cannot be punished in such a way for their actions. Life in prison for a person who does not show themself to have the means to improve and pose no danger to society should suffice, but to end someone's life because of certain biologically based actions that are out of their control just does not make sense to me.

---

1   "State by State," Death Penalty Information Center, 2019, accessed June 20, 2019, https://deathpenaltyinfo.org/state-and-federal-info/state-by-state.

Philosopher Robert Blatchford said in his book *Not Guilty* that if it is true that one does not have free will and could not act any other way in a given situation, then it follows that all praise and all blame are undeserved.[2] All praise, all blame. That is a lot to handle, and the jury seems to still be out on free will, but as long as it is a mystery (and many studies seem to point to us being slaves to our environment and heredity) I cannot, in good conscience, defend or advocate the death penalty.

I don't think there will be much argument that Hell is one of the vilest of religious beliefs. It sickens me to think that people who claim to be good actually believe in and are okay with the idea that the invisible man they worship would torture their children forever if they deny the existence of said invisible man. My very own grandparents believe I will burn in Hell, and they believe that my son, their great grand-child, will burn in Hell if he does not find a path to their God. Where is the morality in that thinking?

The only morality you will find in this thinking is immorality! Anyone who believes someone deserves everlasting suffering because they did not believe in the right god or didn't worship a god correctly is not a moral person.

I find it hard to justify everlasting torture for even the worst of human beings. Even a child rapist, Hitler, Stalin, and all terrible, despicable people unworthy of human dignity do not truly deserve everlasting pain and suffering. Prisons, removal from society, loss of societal privileges, and death (not the death penalty, as discussed above) are all things that end the pain and suffering that could be caused by such beings. There is no reason to wish upon them everlasting torture.

---

2   Robert Blatchford, *Not Guilty: A Defense of the Bottom Dog* (New York: Boni and Liveright, 1918).

Now, to touch again on the child abuse aspect of Hell. This is a tricky area, because it is easy to label this abuse when you are on the outside looking in. However, if you really sit down and think about it, if you are a parent and you, with all your heart, believe in Hell and believe people are sent there, wouldn't it be child abuse to not tell your child about Hell? If you thought by keeping your mouth shut your child would burn in hellfire, it would make you a worse parent than trying to secure your child's eternity.

The reason this is important is that you will have encounters with countless parents who believe this. They will tell their child about Hell, and they may discuss it with your child or you. The incorrect action would be to attack them as abusive. I instead would suggest using a more Socratic method of questioning their beliefs and seeing if you can take them apart from the bottom up. These are the same methods we looked at when dissecting faith.

These parents have faith in Heaven and Hell and honestly believe they are doing the right thing by their child. If you wish to dig deeper into that and maybe help their child out, you will need to talk to the parents, learn what they believe, and work through how that baseless and harmful belief can be removed from their lives.

This sounds like a daunting task, and it is. It may not be a task you are up for, and, even if you are, you may not be successful. But I know some of you reading this right now know a child who fears Hell more than anything on earth and needs someone, somehow, to reach out to their parents and remove this from their lives. We know their church won't be doing it.

Sex, Death, and the Meaning of Life

What Is Morality?

Morality is going to come up a lot when reading the Bible and will be discussed again and again, because, for believers, morality comes from a holy book. When I was a kid, we would read through these stories in Sunday school or at home and reflect on the moral of the story. What did I learn? What about the opposite? What if you read through the stories and picked out what was wrong with them. How would your child handle the situation differently? This will teach your children something they naturally have and bring it out in them: empathy. Empathy is a natural, evolutionary trait we possess as our moral compass.

Many parents in the U.S. rely on the Bible as a moral compass. Is the story of David and Goliath really a moral story? David murdered someone! Is it possible he could have handled this better? As an adult, I think so, but as a kid, I thought David was a hero. Is this the kind of hero kids should have? If David were alive today, he would be the front-runner for presidential candidate for the Tea Party. He has their "shoot first, ask questions later" mentality.

Talk to your children about morality and find what's moral in the Bible (not stealing, not killing), then discuss if these are moral beliefs that are exclusive to religion or if people possess these beliefs independently. Here you can refer to science and primatology. How do other species show empathy and moral judgment? Do chimpanzees or gorillas have morals? Look it up with your kids, and watch videos on the subject. I was raised to think only humans had morality and that it was divine. This is utter nonsense, and we have the scientific evidence to show it.

Religious believers attempt to make everything about morality. However, something can only be moral or immoral in a true sense if it affects others. If I walk up to a person on the street and punch them, it is an immoral action. If I walk up to a pillow in my room and punch it, that is simply an action. There is no consequence to punching a pillow.

The idea that morals are divine and static is troublesome. Thinking of morals as relative or cultural is what has led to the mass avoidance of questioning honor killings, female genital mutilation, and countless other religious acts that most societies would renounce in a second if they were not based on religious beliefs. Teaching your children that morality is universal is an important lesson. If killing your daughter for being raped is wrong in a secular society, then it's wrong in a religious one. (This is not to say all secular laws are moral.)

Immanuel Kant spoke of universal maxims as a way to decide the morality of an action. If everyone on the planet repeated this action, what would be the effects? For example, if I am poor and starving, and I'm in a store and realize that I can steal an apple and not get caught, is that immoral? We may look at this and think, no, if someone is impoverished, they must do what it takes to survive, but Kant would argue it is immoral, because if everyone did the same thing, their actions would have great consequences. Think about rising food costs driving more people into poverty, etc. We must look at the consequences of our actions. What is great about universal maxims is that they are fluid and change with the times, with new evidence and with new empathetic understanding. We have the ability to adapt and grow as empathetic creatures. Religion removes this with its unchanging laws. I say unchanging, yet they change them all the time to their own benefit, claiming to be acting on revelations from God.

Kant also described morality as better than religion. We usually think of morality as a good deed or doing the right thing, but Kant took this a little further. Doing a good deed is always good but is not always moral. You have to look at the teleological aspects of those actions. Why did the person perform them?

In my moral philosophy course in college my professor used an example that goes as such:

Scenario 1: I am standing at the bus stop one morning waiting for the bus to arrive, and a man walks past me. As he steps around me, his wallet drops out of his pocket, and he does not notice. I quickly reach down, grab his wallet, not saying a word.

Scenario 2: I am standing at the bus stop one morning waiting for the bus to arrive, and a man walks past me. As he steps around me, his wallet drops out of his pocket, and he does not notice. I quickly reach down and grab the wallet. While I am standing back up I happen to notice a policeman on the corner just across the street who saw the whole thing. I then turn to the man and let him know he dropped his wallet and return it to him.

Scenario 3: I am standing at the bus stop one morning waiting for the bus to arrive, and a man walks past me. As he steps around me, his wallet drops out of his pocket, and he does not notice. I quickly reach down and grab the wallet. While standing back up, I think to myself that my mom always told me stealing was wrong, and I would not want to upset my mother. So I yell to the man and return his wallet to him.

Scenario 4: I am standing at the bus stop one morning waiting for the bus to arrive, and a man walks past me. As he steps around me, his wallet drops out of his pocket, and he does not notice. I quickly bend down and grab the wallet. I immediately yell to the man, giving no thought to anything other returning it to him—and think that I happen to see a lot of people drop their wallets.

How do we rate these scenarios? I think we can all agree that in *scenario 1*, I did the wrong thing and acted immorally. I stole his wallet. In *scenario 2*, I did return the wallet, and we can all I agree I did the right thing, but Kant would say I did not do the moral thing. My actions were guided not by good intentions but by fear of punishment. In *scenario 3*, I have once again done the right thing. I have returned his wallet, but again Kant would argue that this was not a moral action. I returned his wallet, because I was conditioned to return it and did not want to upset a third party (my mother) by going against her lessons. Kant would argue that only in *scenario 4* were my actions not only a good deed but moral as well. I did not consider reward or punishment for my actions, and I did not think about how a negative action could upset anyone. I simply did the right thing, because it was the right thing to do.

Using this method to gauge morality, how can most religious actions be deemed moral? Theists often do their good deeds for teleological reasons. They are afraid of the punishment of an afterlife in Hell and wish to reap the rewards of Heaven for their good deeds. So while many theists may very well do many good deeds, how many of them would stand up to Kant's test of morality?

Morality is a product of evolution, well understood and gaining more and more evidence through many fields such as neuroscience and psychology. Morality has been removed from the grasp of religion, but various religions are not done putting up a fight to claim it. They firmly believe morality is strictly their domain and try to overuse morality in the case of sex, sexual conduct, sexual relationships, sexual orientation, and gender identification. This leads to cultures like the purity culture and to crimes committed in the name of religion, which, in a secular world, are viewed as about as immoral as an act can be, but under the banner of religion they are seen as heroic. I think Steven Weinberg said it best when he said, "Religion is an insult to human dignity. With or without it, you'd have good people doing good things and evil people doing bad things, but for good people to do bad things, it takes religion."

Good people are driven to do crazy things because of their faith, like blowing up an abortion clinic. It is often the case that the people who carry out such acts are not generally bad people, but they have become infected with the faith virus, and faith can make people do irrational, immoral things.

Religion has actually destroyed morality not enhanced it. It has tried to set rules that cannot be changed (though often are) and removed the fluidity of morality. In the secular world, if we learn a past act is actually harmful to human well-being, we can adjust our moral compass. We can put an end to that act and offer a defense of ignorance for the past. We will not pretend it was once actually moral.

Look at Islam. Muhammad married a nine-year-old girl. At the time, this was not outside of the norm and would not have been thought of as immoral. Today our understanding of childhood, consent, and well-being tells us this is wrong. While Muhammad's action was, at the time, justified by ignorance, today it should be condemned. In many cases, however, it is not. Some religious leaders continue to defend Muhammad's act and will not call it immoral, even condoning it in hindsight and saying, "If it is good enough for their prophet. . ."

Christianity does not get different treatment here. It has condoned rape, slavery, incest, murder, and genocide, just to offer a few problematic examples. I always ask Christians why they would want to be a part of a religion with this history. I understand the same can be asked of citizenship in the U.S. Answering honestly, I am only an American by birth. I did not choose to be an American, and I do not have to align myself with any of its teachings. I can fight to change America from the inside, or I can pack up and leave. At this moment, I have chosen to stay and fight for lasting change, to move away from the dark past toward a bright future.

I believe many religious people feel this way about their religion as well. They believe they can offer a new insight and help change the religion for the better. They can help weed out homophobia, fight for women's rights, etc., but I do not understand why one should. Why hold onto such a belief? When it comes to the U.S., I am not holding onto some belief that what we have is "important." I understand the U.S. is flawed, even for all that is good with it. I am no patriot, no nationalist, and I don't pledge allegiance to any flag; I simply live where I was born and want to make this place as great as I can for this and future generations. Leaving simply means I have given up.

I will look at the pledge of allegiance and U.S. nationalism later; this is not the chapter for it. I do, however, bring it up, because when discussing morality with your kids, your friends, or a stranger, these are the types of things you should have in mind. Are you patriotic, believing deeply in the U.S. and its message? Okay, if so, then how do you defend that against someone who is deeply religious? This may seem like a non sequitur, and in a way it is, but I have not found a meaningful way to treat the topics as unrelated. These questions demand an answer, and to make progress in a discussion about morality, you may find yourself in a position where answering these questions is the only way you can get the discussion rolling.

Morality gets tricky because of the extreme amount of gray area. This should not be a distraction from what we know, though. Abortion is one of the largest gray areas in any discussion about morality, and theists are very quick to raise it.

The argument goes that if an action negatively affects someone else it is immoral, and abortion negatively affects the fetus. There are underlying arguments about whether the fetus is a "person," has "rights," and if the mother can make decisions with regard to that fetus. I think, rather obviously, most atheists agree the decision is left to the mother, and the morality of the issue is not really universal but personal. Some people who are pro-choice would never have an abortion but do not feel that their decision has any moral weight in someone else's situation. I think this is the best way to look at it. I also think this is the best way to teach children about abortion and whether it is right or wrong or if it can even be defined that simply. Some choices have complicated solutions that come down to very personal answers.

When teaching morality, I suggest you focus on what we know and how we learn; discussions about empathy and well-being are the best places to start. Increasing humanity's overall well-being may be the most important aspect of morality. If we can do away with practices and beliefs that diminish the well-being of certain people, such as female genital mutilation, death for apostasy, forcing women to wear particular garments, beliefs that diminish a person's worth and take away freedoms based on sex, gender identification, or sexual orientation, then the lives of those oppressed by such beliefs will be improved without doing anything to diminish the well-being of anyone else.

I wait for evidence that a man's well-being is diminished by a female driver in Saudi Arabia or of how a straight couple's marriage has been ruined by same-sex marriage. When we really dig into these beliefs and their "morals," what we find is a group in power oppressing another group with less power. In religion, this is often men exercising power over women. This stops with us. This stops with our children. Enough is enough! We can no longer stand by and think that because it is happening in another culture, in another country far away from us, we can do nothing about it. We also need to drop the idea that we cannot judge these cultures or that it is ethnocentric to do so.

We can know for sure that in all cultures forcing a girl to be brutally circumcised is wrong and does not increase her well-being. We know that forcing a woman to cover her body from head to toe does nothing to increase her well-being, regardless of cultural beliefs and history. We can speak up. We must speak up, and we must teach our children these ideas are morally bankrupt and should be destroyed.

John Rawls spoke of the veil of ignorance. Imagine you are put behind a curtain. It is pitch black, and you are suddenly unaware of anything about yourself. What color is your skin? What gender are you? Your entire identity is erased. Now, pass laws or moral codes based upon what you know. Would you vote for a law forcing women to cover their bodies if you knew that when the veil of ignorance was lifted you could be a woman? Would you remove a woman's right to drive or vote if you were unsure of your own gender?

Of course you wouldn't. You would make sure when that veil was lifted all laws benefited you. Yet many people do not think this way. In many religions and governments you have privileged, wealthy white men making the rules. They decide who gets what and who is treated how. No rich white man is going to pass a law that affects him negatively. We see this with the U.S. government. Congressmen do not tax the rich as they should be taxed, because that would affect their personal bottom line. They do not pass restrictive laws on male reproductive rights, because those laws would affect them. Instead, they pass laws that affect the poor, women, and racial minorities. They are quick to eliminate the rights of others if it increases their own personal well-being.

This is far from moral. Actions like this fail to reach the bar of both Kant's and Rawls's moral philosophies. The U.S. government acts as an immoral institution at almost every level. This is not how the government was designed, but this is what happens when capitalism is allowed to infect democracy. Capitalism itself is unable to pass either Kant's or Rawls's test of moral goodness.

The Morality of Sex

I was raised in what I have come to describe as purity culture light. I was taught that saving yourself for marriage was the right thing to do, and that sex before marriage was a sin. However, my parents were smart enough to also teach me about safe sex. They hoped I would remain "pure" but knew the world we lived in and wanted me to be prepared no matter what choice I made.

I put the word *pure* in quotes because religion views sex as a very dirty thing and uses the concept of "purity" to demonize natural biological feelings. Those who have sex before marriage are seen as "impure." When you are told that sex will ruin you, you grow up with a much different idea of sex and the value of your body than someone who isn't.

The purity culture is a mostly evangelical Christian movement (also seen in many moderate religious areas) that teaches young girls and boys that premarital sex, oral sex, even some kissing and public displays of affection are impure and are a ticket to Hell. They are told their bodies are not theirs but belong to God. They are taught that impure thoughts are a sin, and that they must dress modestly in order to keep such thoughts from popping into each other's heads.

This goes against everything natural in our species and forces a massive cognitive dissonance among our youth. There is absolutely no way a thirteen-year-old boy is not having sexual thoughts while going through puberty, and instead of helping him understand this change and what these thoughts and feelings mean, he is told to repress them, and that to even think about them will result in endless torture in Hell. Girls are taught that if they engage in sexual activity they will be unwanted by men and by God! This is the degrading message being taught to children today. Your natural urges are disgusting. They are a sin, and if you even consider giving in to them, you will burn in Hell, and no one will want you. You are worthless unless you are "pure."

These churches fight against all forms of sex education in schools except 100 percent abstinence-only courses, in which case you do not talk about condoms or birth control and often lie about diseases associated with sexual behavior and about condom success rates against AIDS and pregnancy.

As a secular parent, I understand the desire to teach abstinence. It is the only way to ensure someone does not get pregnant. However, this is not safe education. Just as should have been the case during my childhood, sex education should include safe-sex methods and honest discussion about all the risks involved in sexual behavior. Facts and myths should be discussed. No weight should be given to the idea of saving your virginity or staying pure. The entire focus should be on being aware of real-life consequences, such as pregnancy and STDs, with real statistics not scare tactics.

Is it any wonder that teen pregnancy rates are higher among religious believers and in highly religious states in the U.S.?[1] If you are not educating teens properly, and they do "give in" to these urges, they are unprepared. They do not know about safe-sex practices, and they can't distinguish between facts and myths, because they have been lied to in an attempt to scare them away from having sex.

---

1   Joseph M. Strayhorn and Jillian C. Strayhorn, "Religiosity and Teen Birth Rate in the United States," *Reproductive Health* 6, no. 14 (September 2009), accessed June 17, 2019, https://www.ncbi.nlm.nih.gov/pmc/articles/PMC2758825.

Young adults who are abstaining from sex because of their religious beliefs tend to rush into marriage. An eighteen- to twenty-one-year-old at the peak of his sexual maturity is going to do what he must to satisfy those urges. When you fear Hell is in your future if you have sex before marriage, you end up marrying the first girl who will say yes. This leaves little question about why the overwhelming majority of those making up the near 50 percent divorce rate in the United States come from religious households.

Sex should not be looked at shamefully; you should talk about it with your child as something natural. However, children need to understand that sex involves risks. We focus a lot of time and energy on pregnancy and disease and forget that even though this is a natural act, it can be very emotional. So you have to think about your actions and how they will affect you and others. Your child may find themselves feeling emotionally ready, may feel they are mature enough, but they need to understand that their partner should also be on that same level. Each person views and holds sex in a different regard. To some (even atheists) it is a very special bond and is only to be shared with certain people. To others, sex is about fun, exploring their bodies and their feelings, and they will not hold it in the same protected fashion as others. This does not make a person a slut. The social construct of someone who is sexually active and even slightly promiscuous as a slut or a whore needs to be thrown out. It is degrading, useless, and almost always aimed at women. It is very rare to find a male "slut." Men are praised for their sexual "conquests," yet women are scorned.

Addressing sex provides a great opportunity to teach about gender equality. Gender is nothing but a social construct of how we think a male or a female should act. Why is there a difference? Why do we care about gender and gender roles at all? As secular parents, we are in a position to educate our kids in a way that smashes gender roles and stereotypes.

The purity culture furthers these stereotypes by defining how men and women should behave and dictating the actions of "real men" and "real women." They remove individuality and a sense of self. They tell you who you are, instead of you telling the world who you are. When you are a child and someone else defines you instead of you being able to define yourself, you lose your sense of identity.

Secularists should be teaching our children to find out exactly who they are and try to interfere in the process as little as possible. We, of course, will keep our kids safe, but I think overall we want our kids to be themselves right down to the core. If they pick up beliefs or social traits of ours, we are proud, but this should be because they have questioned our assumptions and rationally decided that they work for them as well. They should not think, "My parent believes X, so I do too."

While we are breaking down gender stereotypes, we should be talking to our children about sexual orientation. Starting early has its benefits. Young children raised to see various sexual orientations as "normal" won't be shocked to see two men holding hands. A three-year-old can understand when you explain that people love each other. As they get older and understand what sex, love, and relationships are, you can get into more detail about what sexual orientation is, how society views it (hopefully better than today for very young kids), and that sexual orientation does not matter. What matters is happiness.

It should be stressed that sexual orientation has no moral weight. Being straight, gay, bisexual, or any other orientation has no moral implications. A relationship has no consequences on others. If a man loves a man, another couple is unaffected by this. Same-sex love then falls outside of morality. It is the same for marriage. If a woman marries another woman, no straight married couple on the planet would experience any change in their life. A same-sex marriage has no consequences for the lives of anyone else. If a man dates a man one week and a woman the next, the same rule applies. No one is affected by this action; it has no consequences for others. It is not a case for morality.

Another important fact about homosexuality is that it is found in nature. Over 450 species have been witnessed displaying homosexual behavior.[2] This alone shows that it is not the human sexual perversion that many religions claim. It is also not a choice. This should be fairly obvious, but many people still struggle with this. If you are gay and are reading this book, you already understand this. If you are straight and reading this book, you also understand it, even if you don't realize it. I often ask anyone who claims being gay is a choice, "Did you choose to be straight?" This also applies to bisexuals. Far too often bisexual men and women are called sluts or used as proof that sexuality is a choice. Though, again, as with gay or straight, it is simply another form of sexuality with which a person is born.

Again, much of this seems like common sense, but it is worth remembering and teaching to our children. In the U.S., as a whole, we are finally improving our treatment of homosexual men and women, but we still have a long way to go. We must keep this moving forward through our children.

We must also tackle more "confusing" topics. I only say confusing because they are so often misunderstood. We often call ourselves allies of the LGBTQ movement, but we often forget about the T attached to that label.

It is time for us to treat transgender people no differently than anyone else and understand that their equality is as much of a priority as that of any other person. As mentioned before, gender is a social construct. You can identify

---

2   Arash Fereydooni, "Do Animals Exhibit Homosexuality?" *Yale Scientific*, March 14, 2012, accessed June 17, 2019, http://www.yalescientific.org/2012/03/do-animals-exhibit-homosexuality.

yourself as you please at any time, and you have the complete right to do so.

As we fight for equality and pass on these lessons to our children we must also remember sexuality and gender are not black and white. As atheists and humanists, we must remember that part of the purpose of raising freethinkers is that we can abolish the old way of thinking in this country. We can finally start on a path of speaking about the LGBTQ movement in the past tense, because someday the movement will not need to exist, as no LGBTQ individual will be seen as any different from anyone else.

In the humanist and atheist movement, we are traditionally and overwhelmingly accepting of the LGBTQ community, but we need to do better. Where do we need to improve the most? We need to better support the trans community. We endeavor to be amazingly accepting of the "LGB," but we fall short on the "T." I am not sure why this, but I have some thoughts.

When it comes to the LGB, we all seem to know someone, either very directly and personally or indirectly. We understand their struggle, and we want to fight alongside them. However, I think very few have a direct connection to the transgender community, or, at the very least, we don't think we do. Because of the terrible social stigma still attached to it trans people are not as open. Many of us probably do know someone who is transgender, but who is still too afraid to come out.

I think the fact that it is still so hard for the LGBTQ community to come out in so many parts of this country is one of the biggest battles transgender people face, and, as humanists, we will embark in this battle with them, but we have to make sure to include them all, not just those we know. It is our duty as humanists to work toward erasing the social attitudes involving traditional gender roles and create a safe and understanding environment for those who do not fit into our society's current gender norms. No matter how small a group appears (and I say "appears," because I do believe it's much larger than we know, and once we change what society accepts, we will get to know of many more transgender people) we should be fighting for the human rights of its members.

So please learn as much as you can about the transgender community, especially in your area. Reach out to them and offer support through your humanist group or on your own. Find out what you can do for them, and let's be sure to include everyone in our common struggle. L, G, B, *and* T.

Dealing with Death

Death should be taught about as something that is just as natural as birth. It should not be feared. Socrates said during his trial, at which he was sentenced to death, "To fear death, gentlemen, is no other than to think oneself wise when one is not, to think one knows what one does not know. No one knows whether death may not be the greatest of all blessings for a man, yet men fear it as if they knew that it is the greatest of evils. And surely it is the most blame-worthy ignorance to believe that one knows what one does not know."

We know death exists, and our best understanding of it is that it is the end of all cognitive processes and that our memories and consciousness cease to exist. This should help us cherish life even more; this is all we have, and we are lucky to be alive. To quote Richard Dawkins, from his book *Unweaving the Rainbow*, written before he become a problematic figure in the atheist movement:

> We are going to die, and that makes us the lucky ones. Most people are never going to die because they are never going to be born. The potential people who could have been here in my place but who will in fact never see the light of day outnumber the sand grains of Arabia. Certainly those unborn ghosts include greater poets than Keats, scientists greater than Newton. We know this because the set of possible people allowed by our DNA so massively exceeds the

set of actual people. In the teeth of these stupefying odds it is you and I, in our ordinariness, that are here.[1]

My son once asked me what he did before he was born. I told him nothing, he didn't exist yet. When he later asked about death, I said it was just like before he was born, and asked if he remembered before he was born? He looked puzzled and reminded me he was not alive then. So I asked him if he did not remember it, did he feel pain? Of course, he answered no, and I told him that is exactly what death is like. You won't even know it.

That sounds grim, but it's as close a description as I can imagine. You can lighten it up a little by explaining that their matter will return to the flora and fauna that created them, that their cells, what made them what they are, will return to the earth and new life can stem from that. They will indirectly live on forever in nature. Not as exciting as seeing your loved ones in Heaven, but I find it more satisfying. The idea of seeing loved ones again may sound amazing, but since we can reasonably conclude this will not happen, we can look for what amazing things will happen. How beautiful is the thought that someday you will be part of a tree outside? You will nourish the plants or animals and life will continue to exist, in part because of you.

I was once asked if I would tell my own child, if they happened to be terminally ill, that they would go to Heaven. I had to think long and hard about this, and I decided the answer was no. Now, to be fair, if my son said to me he believed he was going to a place such as Heaven, I would not tell him he was not. If a thought like that was his and brought him comfort, I would go along with it. However, I would not bring it up on my own. I don't want to lie to my own child because

---

1 Richard Dawkins, *Unweaving the Rainbow: Science, Delusion, and the Appetite for Wonder* (Boston: Houghton Mifflin, 1998).

making him feel better would make me feel better. If he knows nothing of Heaven or an afterlife, why bring one up? I can say as a parent, though, atheist or not, that I should not pass judgment on whatever decision another parent makes for their child in a situation like this.

When discussing death and Heaven and what the afterlife is, you will also have to discuss the more vile side of religious belief: Hell. Have a long discussion with your child about Hell, what it is and why it's not real. Tell your children, without hesitation, that Hell is a flat-out myth and a lie used to control people. Leaving this topic open-ended is unfair to someone who is unable to completely think about it rationally and critically. No need to keep your child up all night simply because you don't want to overly indoctrinate them with your own views. I was raised believing I could go to Hell if I didn't believe in God or was a sinner. These things kept me up at night. I attended a Christian school for a few years, and this idea was pounded into my head. Sinners burn in Hell for eternity. This idea repulses me, and I would never threaten anyone with such a claim. I cannot fathom a morality that includes believing some people will be tortured for eternity.

Hell has already been covered in this book, so I won't expound further, but a conversation about death cannot take place without speculation on the afterlife. Death is one of the main selling points for religion, if not the main one. It is the believer's fix for everything. Ask a theist about starving kids in Africa, and they will tell you, "They will get their reward in Heaven." Ask them about mass murderers like Hitler, and they will assure you that he will get his due in Hell.

These may sound like reassuring ideas, but it does nothing but turn religion into a death cult, as I mentioned earlier in this book. When you tell someone you don't believe in God, they start to worry about your afterlife. They don't ask much about your actual life or worry about you being hungry or homeless. No, that's only temporary, and that suffering only brings you closer to God. Deal with your own problems in this life, as they cannot be bothered, but the afterlife, oh, you better get on that!

This is also about the time the "What if you're wrong?" question comes up. This question doesn't make much sense to me, because I think, turned around, the question is more important. What if they have been worshiping the wrong god all along or worshiping wrong? If I am right, they won't even know it.

I often get a little snarky here and agree for the sake of argument that maybe I am wrong. Yet if I am wrong and I get to Heaven's gates and it is the Christian God, the God of the Bible, that is standing before me, would I even allow him judge me? My crime is merely that I did not grovel at his feet while he let millions starve, let people suffer from cancer and other horrible diseases, and allowed natural disasters, murder, rape, child molestation, and various other tortuous realities. I make it very clear, if I am wrong, and they are right, I want nothing to do with their God.

I then go into a bit more detail and explain that if I am wrong, in all probability, so are they. While I cannot ever claim absolute certainty that there is no higher power, I feel very comfortable claiming rather certainly that whatever god anyone on this earth is worshiping is a myth. Each and every belief on this planet reeks of a human creation.

I often ask why a Christian isn't a Muslim. There is much more compelling evidence for the existence of Muhammad than there is of Jesus, so wouldn't the Muslim story be more believable? Wouldn't it make more sense that having evidence for your prophet would set your religion above all others?

Death is nothing more than an end. We have for most of human existence tried to make death much more poetic than it is. Everything dies, and we don't expect that every plant and animal goes to Heaven. How crowded would Heaven be. Are Homo sapiens the only species up there? Did any of our ancestors have souls, or did God wait until the exact right animal was born, the one that he believed was the first of the Homo sapiens, and inject a soul into it?

I think life is cheapened if you believe this is only a temporary stop. What are we looking forward to in an after-life anyway? The Bible doesn't say much, if anything, about what Heaven is like, so why is everyone so excited about it? What if it sucks? What if you have to share a house with your mother-in-law? What if it's a nudist colony, or, worse, what if you go there as you died? Imagine all the old people walking around. Okay, I'm kidding, I love the elderly, but really, think about it. If you died at ninety-two, would you really want to be that old for eternity? Of course not. However, churches have done a great job at marketing Heaven as perfection. It is so perfect you can't actually imagine it. It is beyond human comprehension. This is nothing more than story time for adults.

At the end of the day, the best answer we have about death is what science can tell us. Our bodies shut down, our organs cease to work, and we cease to exist as anything but a body. We are then buried or burned, and all that remains of us are the memories our loved ones carry with them.

It may not be a mansion in the sky, but I would much rather know that when I go I will remain alive in the minds of people I have somehow affected, rather than pretend that all the adversity thrown at me in this life is just a test. I would rather push that crap out of the way and live this one life to the absolute fullest.

For centuries, poets and writers have wanted to make death beautiful when, really, it is just the end of something. We cannot be here forever, and death is just the final act we play out as humans. It is one of the few things we can only do once and don't get to try again (I guess birth falls into this same category), and death is remarkably sad. We cannot avoid the sadness that comes with dying and knowing that we will never again see people we love.

I have often, and too morbidly, thought about my own death and how I will have a very hard time coming to terms with never seeing my wife and son again. One of the worst aspects of death for me is knowing that life for everyone else carries on, and I don't get to be a part of it. Yet I find solace in knowing that after I go, I won't know I missed any of it. All the sadness I felt will be gone. This isn't the greatest comfort in the world, but it is some, and it is the truth to the very best of our knowledge.

I would much rather deal with an uncomfortable truth than a lie. I think our children deserve this too. Sometimes reality is not the illusion we want it to be. Even putting aside the jokes about mothers-in-law, of course I would love to know I would spend eternity with my wife and son. I even think the horrors of everyday life may be made more bearable in thinking this way. I can never understand how parents deal with the loss of a child. It is something that scares me more than anything else in the world, so of course believing that death is not the end would bring a great deal of comfort.

I cannot do that, though; I cannot live with a lie. I will not put these lies into my child's head, just because I think they may make life easier. The truth is always better, always, no matter what comfort may be lost. The lie comes at a cost of not being able to appreciate life as we know it. I have said it already, and it can be said again and again: when you look forward to the next life, you devalue this one. No matter how many times a religious person tells me this is not true, I simply have a hard time believing them because of the significance they place on the afterlife.

The Meaning of Life

How does one find meaning in their life? Growing up religious, you're taught that life's meaning comes through God. You read the scriptures and pray you'll discover God's plan for you. So what happens when you realize your prayer and your book are meaningless? This is surely going to be cause for concern for anyone who has embraced these teachings.

Discovering life's meaning is a personal journey that no one can take for you. Even a religious person does not get their meaning from the god of their choice. They get it from within, just like everyone else. They just think they found it in some divine revelation.

Everyone finds their own meaning and their own purpose. Nature does not give our lives meaning, and it certainly won't give us a purpose outside of reproduction. Meaning and purpose are self-discoveries. The meaning to my life is my son, my wife, doing what I can to help anyone and everyone, and to fight to make this world egalitarian and safe for all. This does not have to be your meaning, you could very well find meaning in making people laugh, in hiking in nature, or in feeding the homeless. I could go on for hours about all the different things in which someone could find meaning. All these answers are legitimate. Life is what you make of it. This is all we get, so finding what makes you happy is key, as long as your happiness does not hurt others, you should be doing all you can to be happy.

So teach your children how to discover their life's meaning, and, in all fairness, they may change their minds a thousand times throughout their life. There is no rule that states you cannot change your mind or discover new purposes for yourself in your time under the sun.

When someone asked Richard Dawkins why he bothers getting up in the morning, he answered:

> After sleeping through a hundred million centuries we have finally opened our eyes on a sumptuous planet, sparkling with color, bountiful with life. Within decades we must close our eyes again. Isn't it a noble, an enlightened way of spending our brief time in the sun, to work at understanding the universe and how we have come to wake up in it? This is how I answer when I am asked—as I am surprisingly often—why I bother to get up in the mornings.[1]

That is finding meaning in life: realizing your place in this world and how small the probability that you are here and not someone else. That you happen to be here, assembled in your exact DNA sequence, to enjoy this life is all the "miracle" you will ever need and all the inspiration you should need to find meaning in your short time on the earth.

Do not let your children ever believe that someone else can assign their life meaning. It is up to them. People often believe their personal meaning in life should be pushed on others. Think about the days when you did not have children. Everyone with a child loves to tell you that you are missing out on the meaning of life. What they fail to understand is that this is their meaning not yours, and even if you have children, it does not mean you will simply decide that kids are your meaning. You may have another passion that keeps

---

1   Richard Dawkins, *Unweaving the Rainbow: Science, Delusion, and the Appetite for Wonder* (Boston: Houghton Mifflin, 1998).

you going. This does not mean you love your child any less, as meaning can take on so many different forms.

I find great meaning in being a parent, but I also find great meaning in writing, trying to help others, ending suffering, and eliminating discrimination. Must I choose only one and make that the meaning of my life? I don't think so! I believe I am able to find as much meaning in life as I want and as much as I can. I only get this one life, so why limit myself to one thing that brings me absolute happiness. In fact, many of the things that drive me are things I would love to eliminate from this list. If I could eliminate discrimination, if it no longer existed, I could find more meaning in less or discover new meaning in different causes.

We are freethinkers, and we want our children to grow up to be freethinkers too, so we shouldn't limit their ability or impose what makes us happy on them. It does not mean we cannot encourage them to try the things we love: playing sports, reading, music, acting, you name it, but, if they are not into these things, we shouldn't force it. We should allow them to choose a path that is right for them and simply be there for them to offer guidance and protection. If the meaning they find does not hurt them or others, then we should be encouraging them.

It's fairly ignorant to think any meaning comes from a divine being. When you realize you only have one life to live, you find meaning in everything. You enjoy it more, and you worry less about messing up and how it will affect your life after this one. If I make some poor choices, I may regret them, but I can work to fix them. I don't have the weight of some false judgment after this life. I can always work on improving and bettering myself, because I want to, not because I have to.

If I had to tell my son of one major source of meaning in life, it would be working to improve life for everyone, not simply for our family or himself. While improving their lives gives me amazing amounts of joy, I want to go bigger. I want to improve my family's lives, while at the same time improving everyone else's to the degree that I can.

I find meaning in creating a better world, and I will die fighting for that. If I perish knowing I have improved the life of just one person, then I have not wasted a single second on this planet. I can shut my eyes for the last time knowing I gave it my all, and it mattered.

SECTION THREE

Get Active

Coming Out Atheist

I know many parents and people in general who keep their atheism a secret. When it comes to parents, this decision is usually based on a few factors. They are either living in an area that is unfriendly to atheists and do not wish to put their children or themselves at any risk, or they simply think that being an out atheist will make life harder on their children.

If you are an atheist in hiding for safety reasons, I will not tell you to come out. You should come out when you feel it is safe. Sadly, parts of this country are not welcoming to atheists, and if you are forced into hiding because of this, I hope someday the movement advances far enough that you can come out.

If you are an atheist hiding because coming out might make life harder, I would like to talk to you about coming out, especially if you are a parent. Yes, for some, this may make life a little more difficult. Being out means you have to tell friends, family, coworkers, etc. that you do not believe in God, that you are not religious, and so on.

More importantly, though, is that change comes when numbers grow. Atheism is becoming more and more common, and as more people feel the desire to come out and speak up, the less odd it will be for someone to know an atheist.

It's funny to think that some people don't know, or at least think they don't know, an atheist. Atheists are like aliens to some people. I believe we have a responsibility to come out. When we live in a country and a world where so many atheists cannot come out safely, those of us who can have a duty to come out and change the false image of atheism.

We cannot do this from the closet. Change will not happen if we are all hiding from the world and afraid that we may get poked at or that our kids may be called names in school. We can raise our kids to be smart and ready to combat such senseless bullying. We are not protecting them or teaching them great lessons by hiding who we are. We should never let society dictate who we are.

Do we want to teach kids that they should hide who they are, because others may not understand? I don't think so. I wear my atheism on my sleeve, and as much as I like to think it does not define me, in a society like ours, it very much does. The fact that I am out and an activist means when someone googles my name, they find out all about my anti-religion stance and my rejection of the god claims. I am proud to stand up and say I reject the Christian right's claims about U.S. laws being derived from God. I am proud to say I do not believe in any form of deity simply because I am told I should. I am proud that I use evidence and rational thought to come to my conclusions about the world. This is a pride I hope to pass on to my child, and I think many of you do too. While all our children may not in fact turn out to be atheists, we do want them to come to their own conclusions with pride and to never be afraid to be open about who they are.

Coming out also forms community. When you come out, you make others feel comfortable to come out. When a group of you are out, you can form a bond and take local action. You can attend those PTA meetings in numbers and speak at city council meetings and have people there to back you up. None of this happens when you are all in the closet.

Community makes a world of difference. Change does not happen when people act on their own, or at least it happens rarely. In most circumstances change happens because a group has organized and made their voices heard. The idea of atheism as a movement or community is unpopular with some people. Many stick to the dictionary definition of atheism as nothing more than a lack of belief in gods. Yet this definition does not take into account the growing communities and organizations dedicated to supporting atheist causes like secularism and humanist values. One cannot simply ignore what is happening and stick solely to a dictionary.

Terms like *humanism* and *secularism* are great, but they are just fancy ways of avoiding saying *atheism*. I know there are some secular church congregations, but they make up a very tiny minority of the overall secular movement. When you consider that (what I would imagine is) 99 percent of the secular movement is atheist, you have an atheist movement with a small number of religious supporters.

Now, being out does not mean you have to be the next Richard Dawkins or Christopher Hitchens—let's hope that doesn't happen. Being out does not obligate you to debate anyone or bash religious beliefs. It may mean, however, that you will have to be open about your belief in a public setting or stand up for something that is perceived of as wrong. Maybe you are at a PTA meeting, and the school wants to cut evolution from biology class, because some parents don't want their kids to learn it. You may feel obligated, and perhaps should feel obligated, to stand up and say something. Maybe your child's school is working on an event with a local church or donating money to a religious foundation. You may need to speak up and be the voice that tells them this is wrong.

When these moments arrive, if you are unwilling to be out about your beliefs or lack thereof, you will be useless. How would you feel if your child's school dumped evolution and you didn't say anything? So let's be out, let's be active, and let's create a country where everyone can finally be themselves. Maybe someday enough of us we will be out and atheism will be such a common thing we won't actually have to be so active.

As out and proud atheists, we have a responsibility to fix the problems around us and focus on education and science. Why are these things so important? Let's take a look and find out.

The Christian Right Hates Education

I could write a whole book on the problems of education, and, in fact, many people have. Education is in continual decline in our nation. States like Florida, Louisiana, and Texas have found ways to fund private religious schools with taxpayer money. This removes money from secular public schools and lets the wealthy put their kids into private, well-funded institutions, while the middle working class, the working poor, and the unemployed are forced to send their kids to underfunded, overcrowded public schools.

In the end this is bad for everyone. In public schools you have children in a run-down classroom using outdated textbooks, with little to no modern technology to help educate them. This is a nearly perfect explanation of what it means to say public education is in the "classroom to the factory" or "classroom to the prison" business. In private schools, you have posh students in well-equipped classrooms, with up-to-date textbooks and teachers lying to them about history and science. In many private schools, you have textbooks that remove any mention of the Founding Fathers' secular values. If you are lucky enough to have a science textbook that even mentions evolution (as a "theory" in lay terms), then it most likely has a giant sticker on the inside warning you that "evolution is just a theory among many other competing ideas." At best, you may happen to be told it's true but be so poorly educated on it that you walk away without even a basic understanding. You end up thinking that evolution is teleological and that humans are the master result, and that this was all made for us.

What can we, as parents, do to improve education? How can we help better fund public schools, make sure our children get a fair education, and avoid paying for a private school that will teach against our very values?

While I am someone who sees more value in building movements than relying on elections, I can't deny that local elections can directly impact you and your children. Starting at the local level, vote for candidates who support removing public funding from private schools, avoid candidates who support voucher programs (this is one of the most common methods), and vote for those who are supported by the teachers' union. Avoid conservative or libertarian parties. They tend to believe that education can be fixed through privatization and by capitalism. Outside of elections, we need to build strong support for overhauling education around the country and finally accept that capitalism cannot fix all of the world's problems, education being one of them.

Go to every PTA meeting you can. Be a voice and run for the PTA and the school board, if you can. Meet with your children's teachers to find out what is being taught in their classes. Sadly, we may have to supplement at home. I think this is one reason why I am hearing of more and more secular parents opting to homeschool rather than send their kids to public or private schools. Education has gotten so bad. You can no longer trust that a school will give your child a proper education.

I am personally against homeschooling. I think it lacks the social necessity of school, and as smart as we parents think we are, many of us do lack the formal education necessary to teach all subjects. I may be able to handle history and science, but I certainly don't want my child learning math from me. I think the solution is to help everyone. Homeschooling may seem right for your child, but it leaves behind thousands in need of help. The last thing we should be doing is giving up on the system. We should be fixing it.

The religious fundamentalists are at war with public schools. They want them turned away from secularism and have been fighting since the courts ruled organized prayer in school unconstitutional in 1962. Violence in school is blamed on God no longer being welcome in schools. I always found this odd. They believe in a God who can create an entire universe but can't break the rules of the Supreme Court to intervene in a school shooting. The political right has taken the side of the religious fight against public schools and has worked tirelessly to defund public schooling and put schools on the open market, forcing schools to compete for funding and using vouchers to fund them. Their proposals always have a loophole that allows vouchers to go to private educational facilities as well, and when they do, you better believe that religious schools are benefiting greatly. Former governor of New Mexico Gary Johnson was so successful at implementing voucher programs for the Republican Party that he extended it to childcare and found a way to fund religious childcare institutions with taxpayer money. This is one reason why Johnson was invited to run for president as a Libertarian in the 2012 election. He showed that he had a love for God, greed, and capitalism.

We must fight to keep our public schools funded and secular. Church and the home are the only places religious indoctrination and enculturation should be permitted. I am not thrilled to think that this happens, but parents have rights, and I will defend those rights. However, their beliefs have no place in the public forum, and other children's education should not suffer at the hands of mythology.

Good News Clubs

The religious right is finding ways into our public schools. They sneak in programs such as the Good News Club (GNC), an after-school program run by the Child Evangelism Fellowship. They entice kids into joining with posters advertising fun stories, games, and lots of snacks. Some groups have argued that because parents must give their kids permission to attend a GNC meeting and it takes places after school hours, it does not violate any constitutional laws. This may be true, however, evidence has shown that their recruitment policies are dishonest and that they send kids home with fliers that mislead parents. Moderate Christian parents are happy to believe that their children will be taught lessons about morality and how to be a good person, when their children are, in fact, being taught a very fundamentalist view of Christianity, one that is based on a literal interpretation of the Bible.

GNCs are a clear violation of federal law, allowing religious organizations to lead children in religious services as part of schools' after-school programs. However, GNC has brought its case before many courts and has won under free speech laws. In the case of GNC v. Milford Central School, GNC won by showing that its free speech rights had been violated, because other groups (though nonreligious) had been allowed to use the school after hours with no questions asked, allowing GNCs to move into public schools around the country to teach intolerance to the unsuspecting youth.

GNCs teach kids Bible stories and passages as literal truth. They warn kids that if their parents are not saved and are not living by the Bible's rules, they will be sent to Hell upon death. This is taught to all attendees, including those kids with same-sex parents. They are taught in a public school that their parents are sinners and are going to burn in Hell. Are Good News Clubs actually good for our kids? I think that is an easy "no."

Can we stop Good News Clubs? Not easily. The Supreme Court seems to be on their side for the time being. The battle will be hard fought to keep them out of your school, and they have millions of dollars at their disposal to fight you tooth and nail in court, but that does not mean they get free rein. As parents, if your school gets a GNC, stay active. Monitor their activities, especially during school hours, which is a clear violation of your children's rights. Talk to other parents. Even many religious parents would not condone the teachings and practices of the GNC.

Just because a GNC strong-armed their way into a school does not mean they can do whatever they want. Stay on top of them, and look for them to mess up. When they do, take action. Their proselytizing has no place in a public school, and we can and will defeat them. I will not spend any more time on GNC, as Katherine Stewart offers an amazingly detailed examination in her book *The Good News Club: The Christian Right's Stealth Assault on America's Children*.[1]

The Christian right will stop at nothing to infiltrate our schools and reach our children. We should not pretend for even a second that they believe that Supreme Court rulings apply to them. They are often quoted as saying that they only abide by God's laws, and that the law of man does not apply to them. This is scary on many levels, but especially when it

---

1   Katherine Stewart, *The Good News Club: The Christian Right's Stealth Assault on America's Children* (New York: Public Affairs, 2012).

comes to keeping them away from our kids. They have never shown respect for any other system of belief or nonbelief, and we have zero reason to think this is going to change.

So here we are: desperate to save education and fighting what all too often seems like a losing battle. We join the PTA and attend meetings and struggle to keep a proper secular education intact, yet state and federal politicians are ready to vote down any and all legislation that removes religious influence on education. Bible Belt states are working around the clock to find ways to teach evolution or intelligent design. They are finding coy ways to place religious groups into schools either as Good News Clubs or through other backdoor deals, and that allows them to covertly proselytize to children.

We must be more diligent about who we elect to office—not only in the U.S. Congress but also in city council, state legislatures, as mayor, or as governor. Most education versus religion court cases wind up at the Supreme Court, and the president appoints these judges, who are then confirmed by the U.S. Senate. If we are not careful, more and more conservative judges will be appointed to seats, allowing them to open up our schools to religious teachings. Some may start small, but before you know it, classes could be opened with a prayer—not an inclusive prayer, but one that supports the single idea of the Christian God of a particular version of the Christian Bible. A Christ-based version of history will then replace secular truths, with Thomas Jefferson either portrayed as a God-fearing Christian or removed completely.

The Christian right is ready to rewrite American history and to stand by the myth that the U.S. is a Christian nation. Nothing could be further from the truth. Our Founding Fathers fought to break away from religious persecution and form a secular nation. This historical fact is damaging to the desires of the Christian right, because the more students who are taught the truth, the less ground the religious right can hold.

As parents, we owe it to our children to fight for their education. Americans continue to fall behind in math, science, and literacy. It has become increasingly clear that politicians are not going to make the needed positive changes for us, so we must be the drivers of change. Our children look to us to steer their lives in the right direction as they grow up, and the longer we ignore education, the more we hurt their futures and the future of the nation. The further we fall behind, the less academic opportunity there will be for future generations.

Imagine an America void of scientists, because they had to go to Europe to find work. Imagine an America where groundbreaking cures for serious illnesses are not discovered, and we become the onlookers to such innovation. As we watch the American auto industry struggle to keep up with foreign competition, are we watching the same thing happen in academia? European nations watch, in awe of our ignorance. They see an industrialized superpower arguing over the origins of life and the well-being and equality of its own citizens.

We are becoming a joke, a walking parody of what democracy will become when money and religion are the driving forces. Education is what can change this country, bring back innovation, fix our broken economy, and grow an educated workforce.

The key to overall improvement starts with education. To pretend otherwise is to throw in the towel and lose the fight for our children's future.

The Pledge of Allegiance

The Pledge of Allegiance is a rather touchy topic in the U.S. It is a common misconception among religious believers that "under God" is an original part of the pledge. Few do the actual research to discover that that phrase was added in 1954, yet the pledge itself was written by Francis Bellamy in 1892.

Bellamy's original pledge reads as follows: "I pledge allegiance to my Flag and the Republic for which it stands, one nation indivisible, with liberty and justice for all." It underwent many changes before 1954, but adding "under God" was not one of them. The final change before 1954 is the version we should still be saying today (I say should be and will touch on that later): "I pledge allegiance to the Flag of the United States of America, and to the Republic for which it stands, one Nation indivisible, with liberty and justice for all."

I personally do not recite the pledge, and I will get to that in a minute, but for those who decide to or who send their kids off to a school where it is recited every day, I suggest teaching them the pre-1954 version that omits "under God." We created the idea of a Christian nation in response to the "atheist communism" of the Soviet Union at the beginning of the Cold War, and although the Red Scare and the Cold War are over, we are apparently sticking to the Christian amendment.

I have heard of teachers who get upset when students do not recite the current version of the pledge. Do not be afraid of those teachers, because you have the law and history on your side. Do not be afraid to stand up for your child's right to omit God or to not stand up at all. As I said, I do not stand for the pledge, and though I will leave the decision ultimately up to my child, I will explain why I don't.

It is really rather simple. I am not a nationalist. I do not pledge my allegiance to any flag or country. I was born in the U.S. but couldn't possibly have had any choice in the matter. Simply because I was born within its borders does not mean I owe the U.S. anything, including my pledge of allegiance to it or its flag. I have watched videos of Nazi Germany and have seen millions of citizens swear allegiance to their county, under threat of death. That is not the world I am going to live in. I will not align myself with any nation out of fear, and, frankly, I am rather embarrassed by this country. Our history is shameful, and I would not pledge myself to it for that very reason. Our treatment of Native Americans, witch hunts, slavery, segregation, marriage inequality, immigration policies, privatized health care, and crony capitalism leave me bereft of qualities of which I can be proud.

I am often proud of American citizens for their accomplishments, but I don't think that means I must be proud of the country. If a great scientist makes a discovery, the country didn't make that discovery; it was that scientist. I may be proud of them, and I may be proud of the schools they attended that fostered such greatness. I may even be proud of the government that funded such great projects, if that be the case, but even then I will not swear myself to any one country. I just don't see the point. I fully plan to explain this to my son, so that he understands what allegiance means and doesn't simply accept it because some teacher told him to.

Atheist and secular groups have brought the pledge before the courts without much luck. It really is a case worth looking at, though. Now, to say I think it's worth looking at does not mean I think it's highly important. I would much rather equality and other issues that affect people's lives directly be addressed and resolved first. That being said, I don't think, "little" cases like this should be totally ignored. "Under God" being in our pledge is a violation of our Constitution. It clearly endorses a religion, something our government is forbidden to do. Any judge that honestly cares about upholding the Constitution would see this and rule in favor of removing it. No judge has dared do such a thing. Sadly, in the U.S., Supreme Court justices are political pawns and not nonpartisan as they should be. They seem to answer to the party that nominated them and don't frequently rule outside of party lines. It does happen, of course, but it is rare.

Education is in decline in this country and science is under direct attack from the Christian right. Science is public enemy number one for Christian fundamentalists in the U.S. Science strikes fear directly into their hearts, because they know they are losing the fight against science, and they fear this fight will end their stranglehold on the country. They know very well they are lying to people. They know the myths they are peddling are false, and they know they can only keep it up if they keep the masses undereducated. Teaching our children science is one of the most important things we can do, but that alone is not enough. We also must fight for science education in our classrooms. We cannot be the only source of science for our children. Natural selection should be taught in all middle and high schools. You should not be able to graduate without a basic understanding of evolution, because it is essential to all sciences.

The How and Why of Science

I didn't grow up with a crazy obsession with science. I always enjoyed it, though. *Watch Mr. Wizard* was a popular television show when I was young, and *Bill Nye the Science Guy* came along later. I really liked my science classes and learning about plants and animals. I did, however, spend a few years in a Christian school where science was all but ignored. Evolution, I was told, was not simply a "lie" but was actually an idea discarded and disproved. It was taught to me that scientists once believed this was the best explanation for life, but later evidence proved that God made us all just as we are. We were not taught that it was an evil secular plan, just that it was an idea that had later been thrown away, never to be used again. I remember watching a science video, and they fast-forwarded right past the entire section about Pangaea and the dinosaurs and their extinction. The same video showed us the planets and had depictions of what each planet looked like on the surface, and they all had plants growing on them with beautiful landscapes that looked like an earth with no animals.

I always thought I would be a historian of some sort, but, alas, my journey on this tiny blue planet led me to science through different bumps in the road and explorations of who I wanted to be. Now, as a parent, all I want to do is teach my child science and to also spread my love of science to anyone who will listen.

Science can be the most fascinating thing any parent can teach their child. It can also be a great way to spend time with your child and have fun while learning. I won't write out all the different experiments you could try with your children, as there are already many great books for that, but I will highlight some of the key points in educating your children about science.

Contrary to religious claims, teaching your kid that evolution is a scientific fact is no more indoctrination than teaching them that $2 + 2 = 4$. Explain the big bang, how the stars and planets formed, and compare those to the stories of the world's religions. Do not shy away from calling these stories myths, especially if they are, as with creationism. Again, teaching your child the scientific truth about the origins of life is not indoctrination; it's education. If you told me the earth was square, and I corrected you with evidence, would you call that indoctrination? Of course not. You would thank me for setting you straight about your mistaken views.

Never be afraid to say, "I don't know." If your child asks you a question you don't know the answer to, you can research the topic together. Many children will ask where we came from. They may simply be asking about the birds and the bees, but it could be more than that. They could be asking a question that can be answered by evolution, but they may be asking questions that have more to do with abiogenesis (how life originally formed on earth). This, of course, is still being researched, and there are many great hypotheses, but no theory has yet come to light. This is not a bad thing by any means and is a great lesson for your children in learning the scientific method and how answers are found.

Let's start with some basic scientific terms that will be a great refresher for parents and will be a valuable lesson for children. Many critics of science tend to misuse scientific terms in an effort to debunk claims that do not match their beliefs. We are all familiar with creationist arguments such as "evolution is only a theory." They are either doing this to be misleading, or they do not actually understand the scientific meaning of the term "pure theory."

Hypothesis: a tentative explanation for an observation, phenomenon, or scientific problem that can be tested by further investigation. Meaning, if I take a pen and drop it, it should fall to the floor because of gravitational force (hypothesis). I can then drop the pen (experiment). If the pen drops to the floor, I have confirmed my hypothesis. In reality I would want to test this more than once to confirm it is the same case every time.

Theory: a set of statements or principles devised to explain a group of facts or phenomena, especially one that has been repeatedly tested or is widely accepted and can be used to make predictions about natural phenomena. Because I have tested my pen hypothesis and confirmed it as fact, I can now apply that to the theory of gravity as stated in my hypothesis.

This is what trips up creationists. They have a layman's understanding of the term theory, meaning they consider it an idea or hunch. Scientifically, however, a theory is a factual statement based on evidence. A theory explains a natural event. Evolution is a theory, gravity is a theory, and countless other truths we accept everyday are theories.

Law: a general empirical statement (based on experimental evidence) that seems to always be true. It is worth remembering that theories are more important than laws. When someone dismisses a theory saying it is not yet a law, remind him or her that theories are more valuable.

So I called gravity a theory, but it is also a law. Confused? Well, gravity is a law in the sense that it tells us the size of the gravitational force, but it does not explain why gravity exists or even why it is as strong as it is. The theory itself is part of the theory of relativity. The law tells us what something is but not how it works.

So will evolution ever become a law? No, simply because evolution explains how life on earth formed, therefore it will never be a law. Many of the mechanisms inside the theory of evolution are laws. Creationists tend to be of the mind-set that since it's not yet a law, it is not yet true. This couldn't be more wrong. Evolution is a fact. It is backed by empirical and testable evidence, just like gravity. You don't see any creationists jumping off buildings yelling that gravity is only a theory.

So now that we have some basic scientific terms down, and we have hopefully dropped pens with our kids to explain not only how gravity works but how science works, we can better explain to them how this all comes together.

Let's start a scientific experiment with your child. The first step is observation. I have observed that when I drop my pen out of my bag it falls to the ground. Second, we develop a hypothesis. I believe that if I drop my pen, it will fall to the ground because of an invisible force called gravity. Then we test this hypothesis (the experiment) and drop our pen to the ground. It will fall to the ground. You should repeat this a few times. Write down how many times you try it and the result of each try. You have now collected data. What does this data tell you? You are now responsible for interpreting this data correctly. Is gravity pulling your pen to the ground? Yes! Your hypothesis is now verified.

Of course, this is a crude experiment, and I suggest buying a book full of fun experiments you can do with your child that will challenge them to come up with their own hypotheses and put them to the test. Success and failure are going to be very important parts of this teaching.

So how do we apply science in teaching our kids about our lack of belief in gods? Well, let's start with honesty. I do not know that God does not exist, but I think it's very unlikely. Why? Simple, there is just no need. Your own answers may vary, and you may not believe for a variety of different reasons, but this is my reason. Science plays a big part in why gods are not necessary. Questions that were once answered by claiming that a god did it are now answered by science. How did the universe come into being? The big bang theory can give you some insight. How did life on earth come to exist? The diversity of life on earth is explained by evolution through the process of natural selection. Why do the planets rotate and revolve around their host star? This was answered by Einstein's theory of relativity.

Here is a great place to talk about advances in scientific thought. Religions (and scientists in those religions) once thought the earth was flat, but this has been scientifically proven to be false. So while some theists love to say science was once wrong, it is important to remind them science is self-correcting. Religion refused to go along with the changes in science, while science evolved with new evidence. We know the earth is round. It was once thought that the sun revolved around the earth. Thanks to Copernicus and Galileo, we know that is wrong, and, in fact, the sun is the center of our solar system and all planets revolve around it. It was even once thought that we were at the very center of the universe. As it turns out, this is not true, and we are not even at the center of our own galaxy, the Milky Way. What is at the center of the Milky Way galaxy? All observable evidence tells us it is a black hole.

It is important to show how science advances; it does not stay stuck on one answer if new evidence arises. This is what scientists refer to as a paradigm shift. If new evidence shows a necessity to replace an existing paradigm, the paradigm is replaced. This is not something religion does very well. No matter what new evidence comes to light, believers hold tightly onto their presupposed ideas, which hinders their development. Science is not afraid to bring in new evidence and replace ideas if need be. No scientist wants to see their hard work replaced, but in science to concede to new evidence is a highly respected virtue.

How does science gain such respect? Why should we trust science and scientists over ministers? The answer is peer review, and this is the basis for what I see as almost all the trust in science. Scientists verify each other's data. A scientist cannot make a claim about an experiment, call it a theory, and assume that it will be widely accepted. The scientist will first need to write a paper and submit it to a respected peer-reviewed scientific journal. Other scientists will then have the opportunity to question and verify the findings. If those findings cannot be falsified, then they are worthy of respect in the scientific community, and the paper will either be a part of an already established theory, or, if big enough, it could signify a paradigm shift and bring in a whole new theory.

This bit of information will be crucial to teaching your kids about science, especially scientific theories such as evolution. If creationists wish to sway your child from the truth and sell them on their brand of creation myth, confront them. Your child will know why evolution is a fact that is verified and accepted by scientists around the world.

Aside from the easy to dismiss "it's just a theory," you will also hear "no new species has ever been created," which is a false statement. For example, scientists have witnessed the evolution of a new species, a finch, in the Galapagos Islands.[1] Apart from speciation, evolution has been observed count-less times in the lab, especially in fruit flies. They breed so quickly you can actually witness the evolution of many gen-erations in a very short period of time. This allows research-ers to make changes to their environment slowly (particularly changing food available) to see how many adapt and how this changes the species over several hundred generations.

---

1   Brandon Keim, "Birth of New Species Witnessed by Scientists," *Wired*, November 16, 2009, accessed June 21, 2019, https://www.wired.com/2009/11/speciation-in-action.

As most atheists or skeptics know, many religions have a deep-seated hatred of evolution. To accept such a theory would be to say that the Bible and their version of God are not literal truth. In my experience, this usually makes creation-ists very hostile toward those who don't accept their myth as reality. So teaching your child to respect people, while defending truth, is important. Having a basic understand-ing of science will allow a child to take any claim by anyone (even the nonreligious) and apply scientific reasoning to it. If someone attacks their stance on evolution, they will be able to explain why they accept the theory and move on.

Children should feel confident in their own beliefs (using the word pure belief in a broader sense). Every child (and adult) should be able to question their beliefs and sup-positions to make sure they stand the test of time and argu-ment. If you are not willing to question why you believe something but accept it simply because it has the support of authority figures, then is that belief even yours?

Make time to read new scientific articles about discov-eries or experiments with your child. Even have them find their own, and once a week you can sit down, go over them together, and discuss why you each found these stories excit-ing, how they could be falsified, and what their implications might be. What questions should be asked to make sure these are sound ideas and not pseudoscientific?

Here is a good segue into pseudoscience and how to spot it. This is a lot of fun for children. I can remember taking a critical thinking class where we spent two weeks study-ing pseudoscience and presenting our own pseudoscien-tific research. I did mine on how global warming is good for us, you know, because fewer polar bears meant less human death at the hands of polar bears. I think many in the class who took it only to fulfill a needed credit learned a lot about spotting nonsense when they see it! Homeopathy is a prime example of pseudoscience, promoting, as it does, the idea that water has a memory. It contends that water, which "once had medicine in it" but is now so diluted that it's only water, can heal you because the water "has the memory of the chemicals once in it." Psychics, acupuncture, anything by Deepak Chopra, and the absolute most dangerous of all, anti-vaccination, is all pure pseudoscience.

How can you tell something is pseudoscience? There are a few ways. Can this claim be tested? If the answer is no, then it is not science. Homeopathy is a prime example of this; it cannot pass double-blind study. For starters, if you have a control group and an experiment group, since homeopathy is only water, you are giving both groups a placebo. On a chemistry basis alone, homeopathy will fail that test, because if you test water for the other chemicals claimed to be contained in its memory and you find none, then you are giving both your experiment group and the control group water and nothing else. Keep in mind that if alternative medicine had passed scientific experiments and testing, it would simply be medicine not an alternative.

Another thing to know and teach about pseudoscience is about determining if a claim is too good to be true. Some examples would be an ointment that cures cancer, a super food that cures various diseases, or arranging furniture in a certain way to bring calm and positive energy to your house. If something sounds too good to be true, it probably is, or, at the very least, you should be highly skeptical and research it.

So we have explored science and pseudoscience, but as parents, we cannot be experts in all fields of science nor should we have to be. We pay taxes and send our children to school to learn all they can about science, history, math, etc. We face a dilemma, however, because religious believers are not happy that our schools are willing to teach our children about the origins of life on our planet or the truth about the origins of our universe. They object to any teachings that contradict their religious beliefs and think all kids should suffer a subpar education, because their kid may learn a scientific fact to which they object.

Standardized testing and government policies like No Child Left Behind have left our children behind. Education is no longer focused on helping our kids learn, fostering curiosity, and making them excited about the world. It is about them knowing the exact right answers on a test. For things like math and science, this is terrible. We are now raising scientifically illiterate students who know just enough to pass a standardized test to keep their school funded and their teacher employed. The government has made money the educational motivation of schools. Money is not a good tool to push educational institutions to educate. When they are told that all students need to score X in order to keep the school's funding, they are only going to teach them what gets students to X, not what gets the student motivated.

According to a 2011 Reuters story:

> In 2009, PISA found that fifteen-year-old U.S. students ranked seventeenth of thirty-four developed countries in science and twenty-fifth of thirty-four in math. The same study revealed that the U.S. has among the most unequal performances in the world, with achievement levels highly dependent on socioeconomic status. Low-income and minority communities are especially hard-hit by lack of access to high-quality science resources. The results from the 2009 National Assessment of Educational Progress drive home the severity of the problem, with only 18% of New York City's fourth graders and 13% of eighth graders performing at or above the proficient level in science.[2]

---

2   Margaret Honey, "America Is Losing Another Generation to Science Illiteracy," Reuters, August 23, 2011, accessed June 21, 2019, http://blogs. reuters.com/great-debate/2011/08/23/america-is-losing-another-generation-to-science-illiteracy.

The country that once led the space race and the vaccine charge and developed the atom bomb is now a joke when it comes to science education. How did this happen? How did we lose so much interest in science? While many factors play into it, almost all of them have at least one common connection: religion.

The Christian right in the U.S. has been attacking science left and right and is the largest science denial group in this country. Any science that does not fit their religious beliefs is considered a conspiracy and is disregarded. If they decide something is untrue, they attack science teachers who teach it: evolution, global warming, plate tectonics, you name it. If it doesn't fit their view, it's branded as false, no matter the evidence.

This quote from the DVD series titled *Resisting the Green Dragon*, an anti-science religious video set, has this to say about environmentalism:

> Around the world, environmentalism has become a radical movement. Something we call "the Green Dragon." And it is deadly, deadly to human prosperity, deadly to human life, deadly to human freedom and deadly to the gospel of Jesus Christ. Make no mistake about it, environmentalism is no longer your friend. It is your enemy. And the battle is not primarily political or material, it is spiritual. . . . As Christians, we must actively trust God and obey His word. So when it comes to environmental stewardship, we must reject the false worldview, the faulty science, and the counterfeit gospel that threatens to corrupt society and the church.[3]

Not only is this statement wrong, dangerous, and misleading, it's downright senseless! I mean really, really

---

3   *Resisting the Green Dragon* (Peabody, MA: JaxDistribution, 2013).

senseless! To go as far as to think that environmentalism is an attack on religion is to bring your faith to a whole new level of delusion.

These groups fight to have science that teaches children about climate change removed from classrooms, because they fear it will raise little environmentalists who will then destroy religion. And if we know anything about their God, it's that he cannot stand anyone who cares about the earth he created, just as it says in the Bible, under. . . oh wait, it's not in the Bible anywhere.

This is the same view that these people have about evolution. Evolution disrupts their creation myth, and, therefore, the idea must be destroyed. Science scares the Christian right. Fear makes them do irrational things and believe in even more irrational things, such as the notion that environmentalism is an attack on religion. These irrational fears lead them to lobby for irrational laws and policies. With the Republican Party and its Tea Party counterpart now being wholly owned by the Christian right, it is no surprise that red states are pushing bills that are strongly anti-science.

One visit to the National Center for Science Education website and you will be shocked by the anti-science bills in state congresses at any given time.[4] Those states are looking for every loophole they can to promote their beliefs in a public school. The Supreme Court has already ruled that creationism and intelligent design cannot be taught in public schools, but this has not slowed down the efforts of these states or, at the very least, prevented the removal of evolution from the classroom.

Louisiana governor Bobby Jindal introduced school voucher programs in his state that allowed public tax dollars to be used to pay tuition at private schools. These private

---

4   National Center for Science Education, accessed June 18, 2019, https://ncse.com/.

schools teach that things like creationism, global warming denial, and even that the Great Depression are liberal conspiracies. This, sadly, is just one very common method the right uses to funnel tax money to religious institutions.

Not only are these programs bad for taxpayers, they hurt the public schools that lose funding, the communities whose schools crumble, and, most severely, the students. Not only do they end up with terrible science education, they end up with a terrible education from the ground up.

In Louisiana, Jindal placed about eight thousand poor students from the entire state in these private schools, and the data from the LEAP testing done each year showed that those students scored drastically lower (40 percent at or slightly above grade level) than the state average (69 percent).[5] So not only did he take away funds from public schools in desperate need of funding, he took eight thousand children and hurt their chance of a quality education.

The Christian right will risk your child's future in order to keep their myths safe. This may sound like some strange conspiracy theory, but they've made no secret about it. They openly fight education the whole way and make it very clear that faith is their primary motivation.

---

5   Danielle Dreilinger, "Louisiana Voucher Students Score Almost 30 Points Below Average on LEAP Tests," *Times Picayune*, May 22, 2013, accessed June 18, 2019, https://www.nola.com/education/index. ssf/2013/05/louisiana_voucher_students_sco.html.

Raising Critical Thinkers

It is important that we teach our children how to think critically. It is easy to tell them they should, but it is not as easy to teach them how, mainly because we may not be that great at it ourselves.

How many atheists do you know who are anti-GMO or anti-vaccination? We know there can be smart people who adopt positions that are fueled by emotion, misinformation, or bad research methods. Think back to earlier discussions about vaccinations, when those opposed were flooding you with links that were never links to scientific studies but always to blogs or "information" sites from doctors who seemed to be selling a cure-all at the same time they were telling you to avoid modern medicine. This is a failure in critical thinking and is usually the result of confirmation bias. If you start off with the notion that vaccines are dangerous, you will be drawn to articles that confirm your position. Instead, developing a position should begin with a clean slate. This is not easy, but it is crucial.

Ask the question, "Are vaccines safe?" From there, look for information from trustworthy sources and see what they say. What do medical peer-reviewed journals have to say about vaccines? What do medical organizations say? What do opponents think, and what are their sources? Are their sources as reliable as those used by medical professionals?

This very method applies to religion. Who is making the claim, and does the claim defy the laws of nature as we understand them? Is there a simpler explanation for what happened? Is it possible what is being claimed happened?

Look at Noah's flood, with two of every animal on the planet and a handful of human beings on a single boat. Look first at the logistics. How big would the boat need to be, and how much food would be required? What about the carnivorous animals? If you only brought two of each, what did the lions eat for an entire trip? This alone makes the story seem more than unbelievable, but then look at the scientific evidence. Have we found a boat that could have done this? Surely a boat of its size must have left some rather impressive remains somewhere in the world. How about the placement of animals? Did Noah go around and drop each animal off at its particular continent after the flood waters receded? How did he do this?

Then, we can look at the archaeological evidence. Fossils form best in wet conditions. Just imagine the archaeological gold mine that would have been left behind from this massive flood that drowned billions of creatures. What have we found? Well, to date we have found nothing that reflects a flood of this magnitude. In fact, every fossil we have found is just as we would imagine it to be with no flood.

It seems fairly reasonable to conclude there was no flood and no mass killings of people and animals. This is nothing but a myth and can be treated as such. Thinking critically, it was rather simple to arrive at a logical conclusion about this issue.

This can be used for every tale in the Bible. From talking snakes to virgin births, we can look at these stories and apply the same critical thinking skills to them.

Our children should be using this method every day in all matters of life, with claims from friends, family, parents, and teachers. They should be well prepared to question everyone and everything. Doing this also allows them to become their own person and not simply who people are telling them to be.

I think many of us, especially those who grew up with religion, had it ingrained that questioning claims is frowned upon, and that God has an exact plan for who you should be. Many people never break out of that cycle, allowing those whom they consider authority figures to dictate how their lives should be led. The generation we want to raise would be a generation in which nothing is beyond question, from religion to the government, and even to science.

It is often imagined that we cannot question science, but the core of scientific research is questioning. That is what peer review is all about. Often theists, especially creationists, claim we all have faith in science or call science a religion, arguing that we simply accept what scientists say. This could not be further from the truth, and, of course, we know this. This is something important we should be teaching our children. The method whereby we apply critical thinking to science, the scientific method and the rigorous testing scientific ideas are put through, ensures that only sound ideas are accepted as scientifically valid, and that all the others are discarded as nonsense or failures.

Pseudoscience exists because some people lack the ability to discard disproved or untestable ideas. From homeopathy to astrology, science discards claims, and yet people insist on continuing to believe these claims. People who hold on to these ideas and continue to believe them are lacking in critical thinking skills.

We already discussed how to spot pseudoscience, but it bears repeating here, because pseudoscience is such a strong example of the dangers of neglecting critical thinking in real life. How many people need to lose a battle with treatable cancer because they believe nonsense claims by alternative medicine practitioners with an end-all cure that has never been tested or, if it has, failed?

The Burzynski Clinic in Texas offers such a service, despite FDA warning that its treatments are not only unapproved, but that its advertising and claims are deemed to be unlawful. They have been sued for misleading patients, for insurance fraud, and for not being up to state medical standards. Yet they remain open for business, offering a cure that is too good to be true. People who are not using critical thinking skills and who love claims that are too good to be true continue to throw their money at these frauds, no matter the results.

This fraud continues across the globe, and religion has found a way to capitalize on it. This is another reason why critical thinking is so crucial to our children's lives.

How many televangelists have we seen in our lifetime who can heal those who cannot walk, heal the blind, or help someone overcome addiction by placing their hands on their head, yelling loud prayers or speaking in incoherent "tongues," and then, *boom*, they are healed, up walking and dancing, while the audience goes crazy and throws money at the pastor and church to continue this miraculous healing.

This is all a fraud. Everyone involved is in on this secret, and they have discovered that people want to believe in miracles. They want to believe so badly that they will suspend disbelief to do so. We are eager to believe in things outside the laws of nature, and we love the paranormal, even though many of us know that no evidence ever supports such claims.

It may be crazy, but think about it. How many people do you know who do not believe in God yet seem to think ghosts are possible? Maybe it's you. But how could this be? You don't believe in a soul or afterlife, yet you believe we somehow stay alive after death or some energy of ours sticks around. Even we skeptical thinkers can fall victim to thoughts like this. We seem to be evolutionarily primed for it.

Our Struggle for Equality

I hate that I feel the need to write a chapter on equality. I almost feel as though equality should not be something we need to talk about but something that just happens. Sadly, that is not the world we live in, and the struggle for equality is something we must teach.

I should start by saying that I don't personally struggle for equality, because I am privileged. I am a straight, white male, and I am cisgender, which means the gender with which I identify is also the gender with which I was born. I don't have to worry about racial profiling. I am less likely to be arrested on drug charges, and, if I were, I would be less likely to see any prison time. I am more likely to get a job than candidates of a different skin color or gender. I have it easy, so to speak.

What I do have, though, is awareness of having this privilege and an even greater awareness that I live in a country where millions of others do not. I live in a country where a black male is more likely to be sentenced to prison time for a nonviolent or victimless crime than am I. I live in a country where women are going to make less than me at the same job, even if they happen to be more qualified than me. I also live in a country where the government does not try to pass laws limiting my reproductive rights as a male but will do so to women with self-righteous enthusiasm.

Thankfully for me, at a young age, I was taught about inequality, and I was told I had it good. I was never under the illusion I was struggling. Thinking back now, even when my family was struggling, when my dad was on strike and money was not coming in regularly, my parents never let on. I never really knew what it was like to be poor, even if maybe at one point we were.

While I don't believe in luck, *lucky* is still a good word to describe my life growing up. I hope I can provide that same for my son, but at the same time I know how important it will be for him to understand that not only around the world but in his own backyard, people are not so lucky and are struggling.

Race

America has a racism problem. We may not think so. We may think that in twenty-first century racism is a thing of the past. Our grandparents may be a bit racist but not the new generation and most certainly not our kids' generation. This, however, is, sadly, just an illusion; racism runs deep in this country.

African Americans make up about 13 percent of the U.S. population, according to dosomething.org.[1] African Americans make up 14 percent of the U.S.'s monthly drug users, yet 37 percent of Americans arrested on drug charges are African American.

According to Gallup, in 2013, only 86 percent of the U.S. population approved of interracial marriages.[2] That means 14 percent of the nation still thinks there is something wrong with interracial marriage. Fourteen percent may seem like a small number, but that's an estimated forty-one million people, and remember, 14 percent is 1 percent greater than the estimated population of African Americans in this country. So, yes, they are a minority in the country, but 14 percent still asserting that race should be a factor in marriage is frightening.

---

1   "11 Facts about Racial Discrimination," dosomething.org, accessed June 18, 2019, https://www.dosomething.org/us/facts/11-facts-about-racial-discrimination.
2   Jeffrey M. Jones, "Record High 86% Approve of Black-White Marriage," Gallup, September 12, 2011, accessed June 19, 2019, http://www.gallup.com/poll/149390/Record-High-Approve-Black-White-Marriages.aspx.

One issue our country faces is that we are unable to admit we have a problem. We don't teach our children in school that our country was founded on the protection of white men and their property. If we are unable to own up to that, how can we admit we have a problem now? We look back in shame at slavery (well, not all of us), and we admit that this was a bad time for our country. This country had never been more divided than at that time. And the evidence is all around us that in the South those wounds have yet to heal. For all intents and purposes, the South has never gotten over losing the war.

To this day, many in the South call the Civil War "the war of northern aggression," and they don't look back at history and think they were wrong. They think we took from them what was theirs! "The world shall yet decide, in truth's clear far-off light, that the soldiers who wore the gray and died with Lee were right" is inscribed on a monument to confederate soldiers in South Carolina.

What do you say to this? A memorial statue in a U.S. state, a state where all races are free to live, in a country were discrimination is illegal, or so they say, claiming the South and the racist General Lee were right.

This is a second America. This country is still deeply divided. We may not be fighting over freeing slaves, but we are fighting over race relations, gender relations, sexual orientation, the definition of freedom and liberty, and the place the Bible has in our government.

If it wasn't for the good people I know who live in the South, (hell, I am from Baton Rouge, Louisiana, myself), I would be advocating very strongly for a full succession from the southern states.

Sometimes, I think that is inevitable. I sometimes think this country is too large for its own good, but I fear such a succession would mean terrible things for minorities, and not just racial minorities but also women, homosexuals, transgender people, atheists, liberals, Muslims, Jews, or anyone who is outside of what white Christians view as acceptable. The South would become the Iran of North America if they were able to break away from the U.S. Constitution.

The South, of all of America, has the deepest problems with racism. From border cities in Texas to Cuban immigration in Florida, the xenophobic attitudes ingrained in the minds of America's southerners start at the youngest of ages. Race is seen as a defining trait not a mere skin color.

It is lost on so many people that race isn't real; DNA does not determine your race. Society does, because race is a social construct. To say race is socially constructed should not diminish its importance in our culture, and, by importance, I mean the real-world implications of this construct. We may be able to say race is an illusion of sorts, but this means nothing in a country where discrimination based on skin color runs rampant.

What consolation is it to a black man sitting in jail for a crime that would earn a white man a slap on the wrist that his race is a mere social construct? None at all, because no matter how socially constructed his race, in this country, right now, his race matters, and the consequences he faces based on the basis of his skin color are real.

To quote Jason Antrosio, professor of anthropology at Hartwick College, writing on his blog *Living Anthropologically*:

> Social constructions are very real, and to say something is a social construction is not to be equated with illusion or fiction. It also misses the point that some social constructions are more powerful and with more far reaching consequences than others.[3]

---

3   Jason Antrosio, "Social Construction of Race is a Conservative Goldmine," *Living Anthropologically* (blog), March 28, 2018 [August 24, 2012], accessed June 18, 2019, https://www.livinganthropologically.com/social-construction-of-race.

Social constructs are all around us. We will look at another one—gender—shortly. In the U.S., we classify people by their race. It seems odd that we care about this on almost every form you fill out, but we put a lot of weight on race, doing little to adjust for exactly how many "races" there are and how many one person could possibly be. Quoting again from Antrosio's *Living Anthropologically*:

> Most people in the U.S. think they use skin color to classify races. U.S. categories relate to skin color, but not exactly. If it was actually about skin color, racial classifications would look more like Brazil, with lots of different terms and gradations. If it were about skin color, then people might change race classification over the years, or children from the same parents could be classified as different races.
>
> In contrast, the traditional U.S. system is known anthropologically as hypo-descent: children get the racial classification of the parent with the least socially desirable classification. Barack Obama, Halle Berry, and some of Thomas Jefferson's descendants are considered black. The most extreme example is the "one drop rule," that any black ancestry meant being classified as black. There have been recent shifts in these attitudes, and there have been regional and historical variations, but this system remains dominant.[4]

In the United States, you could be 1 percent African American, but if your skin color is dark because of dominant genes, you will be classified as African American and experience an entirely different world than a white person.

---

4   Jason Antrosio, "Race Reconciled: Race Isn't Skin Color, Biology, or Genetics," *Living Anthropologically* (blog), March 26, 2018 [June 5, 2011], accessed June 18, 2019, https://www.livinganthropologically.com/biological-anthropology/race-reconciled-debunks-race.

Our only hope of putting an end to this way of thinking is through education, and while we fight to make this sort of teaching commonplace in our classrooms, it will be up to parents at home teaching our children that no matter what anyone's skin color, they are the same, biologically, physically, intellectually, you name it. Now we know everyone is different and everyone is unique. This is what makes people who they are, but we must understand that it is not their skin color in particular that plays any role in their uniqueness.

Here we must be careful, since so much weight in our country is currently put on race. People do identify their race as part of who they are and what makes them unique. We should never take anything away from that and should support the identify anyone chooses for themself, but to identify and own your skin color in any way that you choose should be an individual's choice not something forced on them by society.

Gender

The Christian right has a real problem with gender. What you see is that they don't understand the difference between sex and gender. You are born, in most cases, with a distinct biological sex (I say "in most cases," because intersex children are born from time to time), and how we deal with that could be a topic of a whole book. Should parents and doctors be choosing the sex of a child?

I digress, however. Returning to the subject at hand, gender suggests socially assigned roles for a biological sex. We condition children to believe girls play house or with dolls and boys play with guns and footballs. We are taught this. It is not biological. We are not born as males with an aversion to dolls. My wife and I worked to avoid this. We bought our son lots of different kinds of toys from dolls to footballs and cars to a kitchen set. He is able to pick and choose what he wishes to play with and is less guided by social conditioning. I say less guided, because I don't know if this can be totally avoided. The same goes for our daughter. Yeah, she loves her dolls, she loves to pretend to cook, but she will drop these activities in a second and play with a Spiderman action figure. We simply do the best we can to let our children grow up and form their own roles in society and choose their own gender identity.

Gender, like race, is a social construct. Like race too, this does not mean gender is not real. Because in our society we place value on gender, often unfairly, people dealing with gender-based discrimination care very little that anthropologists and sociologists call gender a social construct.

Gender discrimination is an alarming problem. We have such strict rules in our society, many unspoken, about gender and the assumption that everyone must have one and must abide by its rules. When a man or a woman decide their born sex and assigned gender do not fit who they are, they should, in an open and equal society, be able to change and live their life as whatever sex or gender they choose. In reality, gender could even be seen as fluid. Why shouldn't someone be allowed to wake up one day, toss on a dress, and live the day as a female and the next day wake up and want to be a man? Why do they even need a gender at all? How does this hurt anyone?

Sadly though, life isn't that simple. There are so many stigmas around gender that anyone who tries to change theirs must overcome countless obstacles, and will face harassment, discrimination, death threats, and even potentially death. Add to that the fact that transgender people suffer from a higher suicide rate than their cisgender counterparts.

Laws are not set up in this country to accommodate fluid gender or gender changes. To change from one gender to another can be traumatic enough without having to first get permission and then fill out paperwork to have your new gender legally recognized, to change your name, etc.

It is time we teach that gender cannot be forced but is chosen. Gender fluidity means gender equality. It means we drop all the social stigmas assigned to gender, and maybe someday we can drop the whole idea of gender and just be people.

Sexual Orientation

The most debated topic in our nation today might well be the rights of homosexual citizens. In the twenty-first century, we are arguing about who can marry whom, while people around the country who have not eaten a decent meal in days, if not weeks or longer, are going to bed in cardboard boxes.

We are a country that cares more about what the Bible says about sex than what the Bible says about poverty. This seems odd, considering that the number one topic discussed in the Bible is poverty, yet the Bible's followers do almost nothing to end it.

The scientific consensus about sexual orientation is that we are born with it, though this should hardly matter. Even if sexual orientation were a choice, what two (or more) consenting adults do together is not your business or the state's business. If two adults wish to be married, so be it. You do not have to agree, but you shouldn't oppose it legally.

Let's be honest. How many parents around the country would do anything to stop their kids from marrying the wrong person in a heterosexual marriage? They don't have the right to do so, but for some reason the Christian right thinks it has a right to stop you if the person you are marrying is the same gender as you.

They treat marriage as a moral issue, but it is not. Marriage cannot be a moral issue, because it has no consequences on any party other than those who are willingly involved. How can the religious right claim there is a moral issue when a marriage on the other side of the country has zero effect on them? It makes no sense, yet our government falls for this every time. We seem to have decided marriage is a moral issue, and since a certain portion of this country thinks homosexuality is immoral, they continue to argue that same-sex marriage should be made illegal once again.

Politicians have a very warped understanding of homosexuality and a preschool conception of what it even means. Former Minnesota congresswoman Michele Bachmann claimed that same-sex marriage would lead to schools being "forced" to teach students that homosexuality is normal and natural. As if that's a bad thing? She even called homosexuals an aspect of "Satan." Again, she's not making it sound too bad.

Rick Santorum, a former presidential candidate, worried that allowing adults to have consensual sex in their homes gave them a right to incest and polygamy. The small government folks in the Republican Party don't want the government regulating big oil, but they want laws that restrict what two adults do in their bedroom.

The Christian right and the Republican Party seem to believe that America's entire foundation will crumble if two men are given a piece of paper that affirms their love for each other. They have so little faith in the strength of the United States that they believe two penises in one marriage will bring the whole thing down.

It's a funny position to hold when almost 50 percent of heterosexual marriages end in divorce, tearing a child's family foundation apart and really messing up the Christian right's whole "traditional marriage" argument.

The hypocrisy is that marriage in the Bible is not defined as narrowly as our government tries to define it in law. Concubines and polygamy are common throughout the Bible. So why isn't this part of our tradition? I also beg of any believer to quote a single time Jesus mentioned same-sex marriage. Find this in the Bible and win a prize. I won't be giving out any prizes anytime soon, because Jesus didn't mention it once, but poverty is cited somewhere around two thousand times. I guess it would be a stretch for the Christian right to use the Bible to better the world, instead of their regular mission of oppressing those they just don't like.

I think telling secularists and atheists to raise their children to be open-minded and to fight for equality could be considered preaching to the choir a bit, however, sometimes the choir needs a reminder of what is happening outside. We have made amazing strides for the rights of the LGBTQ community, but we have a long way to go, and with an ever-changing government of tyrants, it won't take much for it all to fall apart.

Women's Equality

A discussion about equality cannot take place without mentioning women's rights. Women are often the targets of mass discrimination, from control over their own bodies to how much they are paid, and even for many years, their right to own property and to vote. Even today, many religions treat them as subservient to men.

It was the Married Women's Property Act of 1839 that that began to open the way for women to actually own their own property. It wasn't until 1920 that women had the right to vote in the U.S. The movement for equal rights for women in the U.S. during this era was known as the women's suffrage movement. Thanks to the work of brave feminist activists such as Susan B. Anthony, women gained increasing power in the United States.

Sadly, there is still a need for a strong feminist movement in the U.S., because regardless of U.S. law, women are far from being treated equally. In 2019, the female-to-male earnings ratio was 0.80, meaning that full-time, year-round female workers made 20 percent less than their male counterparts.

How are we allowing women who do the same jobs as men to make so much less money? There are laws against this sort of discrimination, yet it continues to happen everywhere. Many try to blame this on women's choice to have their families before returning to the workforce and men staying at work and gaining more experience. This is, of course, nonsense. If this were the case, the pay gap would be almost invisible as not all women make this choice to stay home. Many do have kids and continue to work or do not have children.

So why is there a pay gap? Sexism is one explanation, and yet many other societal factors play a roll. Congress continually fails to enact laws that level the playing field for women. *Egalitarianism* seems to be a dirty word in Washington, DC. There are also other factors at play like the fact that the corporate world is still a men's club, and men pay other men more, apparently trusting other men more and having a skewed view of a women's abilities. However, studies have also shown that women tend to ask for less money in salary negotiations. Another popular belief is that we tend to raise girls to think less of themselves. Often, religion and other cultural factors within the U.S. serve to undervalue women, and so they are raised thinking that they are weak or that they are second-class citizens. This could, hypothetically, lead them to feel as though they are not worth as much as they are and ask for less money. Regardless of whether or not this is the case, I think it's safe to say that as a whole we treat women as inferior to men. There has been great improvement, but much remains unresolved and continues to affect the working world and other aspects of life.

This skewed view is taught not intrinsic. From a very early age boys are taught to coddle girls. Girls play with dolls and cook in pink kitchens, and boys play in the mud with sticks and toy guns. We are conditioned to be overly gentle with girls, because they are considered delicate. We hold doors, not simply to be polite as we should for anyone but for women specifically, with the idea of female frailty in mind. I have never fully understood this one, but maybe our parents thought women's arms couldn't hold doors?

If we teach our kids that girls are delicate and can't handle roughhousing or hard tasks like opening doors (sarcasm), how can we trust them to run a business and work as hard as the men who grew up in the mud? We are simply not raised to think of girls as equal to boys. We must change this.

We should be raising our children to make their own rules. Girls can play in the mud, and boys can play with dolls. Girls can play rough and so can boys, and both need to know where they want to draw the line. Maybe a particular girl doesn't want to wrestle in the mud but another does, or one boy prefers to cook on a fake stove instead of melting G.I. Joes with a magnifying glass.

If we teach our kids that all the other kids are their equals, that is what they will grow up thinking. This seems like the easy part. We know that this will mean that as each generation comes along, the opposite sexes will treat each other better and better. But tackling wealth and pay inequality isn't something we should wait for future generations to do; these are things we should fight for now. However, the whole issue falls beyond the scope of this book, so I will leave it at that.

One of the biggest issues around equality for women in the U.S. is abortion rights. Many Republican states are currently passing extreme legislation restricting women's access to reproductive services in an attempt to get the Supreme Court to once again rule on abortion and dismantle Roe v. Wade. These legislators are pushing a bill they know will never become law, but they also know that court orders and delays will eventually force the Supreme Court to get involved. This strategy is brilliant when you think about it. Most religious leaders understand the Supreme Court can't just overturn a previous decision, and they also understand that it would be career suicide to try in one swoop to outlaw abortion. So the strategy has become one of removing abortion rights piece by piece until Roe v. Wade is rendered meaningless in the face of new legal precedents.

Now, I'm not going to tell you what to tell your kid about abortion. You can be for or against it and be a secularist, an atheist, etc., but I will say that regardless of your personal beliefs about abortion you have no right to impose these beliefs on anyone else. This is the meaning of *choice*. Being pro-choice does not mean that you are personally for or against abortion. It simply means you are for a person's individual right to make a choice on the issue.

This is how I think we should be raising our children. It is your right to tell your children you don't think abortion is the answer to pregnancy, but you should allow them to make up their own minds. You should also make sure they understand that what you are saying is nothing more than your personal opinion, and it should never imposed upon anyone else.

The Republican Party is ready to impose laws on women that are based solely on the Bible. Women would the property of their fathers or husbands. One can only imagine how long it will be before they attempt to bring back a dowry. "You can marry my daughter, but I want an Xbox and two dirt bikes."

Also, when the Christian right questions the legitimacy of a rape claim, they are entirely denying women any trust. Suddenly, we have to question a woman's claim, because obviously no man would rape a woman without good reason, right? It would be totally unheard of for a man to commit an act of violence against a woman, so we must question these harlots' claims. This is the environment that the Christian right is creating. This is the environment we must make sure our children are not a part of.

We should also be raising feminist children, male and female. I do not mean to say that every child we raise must be a radical feminist, but they should be aware of the women's equality issues of their time. Feminism is an important and vital movement that will be around until it is no longer necessary (if that day ever comes). Raising children who fully support feminist or women's rights causes and being open feminist allies means we can help advance these causes.

Creating children who support overall equality is the main step toward eliminating the need to have this conversation over and over again with each successive generation. I hope this will be the last generation that needs guidance on how to treat each other on this planet. We may not be able to achieve this, but I cannot help but try.

Antifascism and the Rise of Neo-Nazism in America

Honestly, this is not a section of this book I would have imagined writing when I decided to write a book about parenting, however, the rise the Nazis, fascists, and all the other far-right groups has made this a topic in my daily life. When something is this much of a factor in the news, you better believe it becomes part of household discussions.

Unfortunately, the far right has gained massive momentum in the last decade, and with the 2016 election of President Donald Trump, they felt even more emboldened. So much so that after the thirty-two-year-old leftist activist Heather Heyer was murdered by a white nationalist during the 2017 Unite the Right protest in Charlottesville, Virginia, the president went on national television and claimed that there were good people on "both sides." Yes, the president of the United States said there were good people on the side of the Nazis. Nazis! He had less to say after another white nationalist in Portland, Oregon, killed Ricky John Best, Taliesin Myrddin Namkai Meche, and seriously injured Micah Fletcher, after the three men stood up to the killer on train while he was harassing two young woman of color, one of whom was wearing a hijab.

It's not easy to talk to our kids about death, but even harder to do so when the deaths are so nationally publicized, so violent, and are caused by groups that are seemingly everywhere in the country and only growing stronger.

This gives us the opportunity to further discuss some of the topics we touched upon earlier. Race, sexual orientation, and gender have a lot to do with the neo-Nazi and fascist ideology. This also opens up a window for us to discuss how to talk about combating such ideas and how we stop these groups from gaining more power and putting more people's lives at risk.

The antifa, short for antifascists, have been very effective in stopping the rise of the fascist right. I won't go into the history of antifascism in this book; you can read Mark Bray's amazing work on this topic, *Antifa: The Antifascist Handbook*,[1] but what I will touch on is how we can talk to our kids about antifa and better understand the work they are doing.

As many people have stated, most of antifa's work is nonviolent. They spend a lot of time online or working inside these groups gathering information, doxxing members, exposing them to their employers and/or communities, and more or less making the world an unsafe place to be a Nazi. Many members of the far right don't want people to know who they are. They know their families will reject them, they will lose their jobs, and their communities will run them out. Doxxing has actually been one of the best tactics used. Antifa have also infiltrated these groups and helped to split them apart from the inside.

I want to go back and touch on the "most of antifa's work is nonviolent" statement I made in the previous paragraph. You see, I would actually argue that none of antifa's work is violent. My reasoning will also help you when discussing what our kids are seeing on TV and help dispel the idea that antifa is "using violence" to stop fascism.

The truth is, antifa is a reaction. Antifascists are not holding rallies, they are showing up to white nationalist rallies. Antifascists are not looking for a fight, they are

1   Mark Bray, *Antifa: The Anti-Fascist Handbook* (Brooklyn, NY: Melville House, 2017).

instead using their bodies as walls to stop fascists from marching in the streets, or as was the case in Charlottesville, they use their bodies to stop fascists from hurting religious leaders like Cornel West, who credited antifa with saving his and other religious leaders' lives when fascists tried to attack them as they formed a peaceful barricade at a park.

These protests have more than once become violent, but antifascists have engaged in defense not offense. They arrive prepared to stop fascists by any means necessary, and self-defense is never off the table. If a woman were to attack her would-be assailant, we would not call the woman violent. We'd applaud her self-defense and be thankful she was able to fight off her attacker. This is much like what antifa are doing. They are showing up, not with an intention of fighting but prepared to defend themselves if attacked.

We don't want our children going out and attacking their bullies, but we also don't want them to let the bullies pound their faces in. Sure, they can tell a teacher about a threat, but that doesn't mean the punch isn't still coming. Antifascists warn cities and officials all the time about the threat these marches pose. However, law enforcement usually ends up joining with the fascists and beating up antifa.

Yet, even if you believe this should be called violence, the argument can and should be made that this violence is justi-fied. You're talking about opposing a group of people whose political ideology begins with mass genocide and ends in a white ethnostate. Even if you did go around hunting down Nazis and fascists and attacking them, you'd still technically be committed to self-defense, because their ideology is, at its core, violent. So even if we use the word *violent*, we can still discuss this with our kids openly. Antifascists are stopping mass violence by standing up to those who wish to carry it out.

We know antifa use diverse tactics, and that couldn't be a better segue into the discussion of dealing with problems like bullies, etc. We know our children will encounter bullies, and we want them to stand up to them in some way, shape, or form. Is that reporting their intended actions to the school? Is it putting their body in front of a bully who is harassing someone who can't defend themself? Is it punching back if a bully comes at them violently? Honestly, it's all of these things and more.

Like antifa, we want our children to do what's right in the circumstances they find themselves in. Different methods work for different situations, and we want them to be smart enough to know when to use which of the tools they have at their disposal.

The Christian Right's Stranglehold on American Politics

It is impossible to write a book about religion in the United States and not talk about politics. I tried not to include a chapter specifically about politics, but, as you can see, I failed. While this chapter won't offer much in the way of how to raise your child politically, because that would be silly, I wanted to write about politics, because it is a major part of the future we are creating for children.

Religion has taken over our political system to the degree that referring to America as a theocracy is not out of line. We are moving further and further away from the secular nation our Founding Fathers envisioned, and this has dire consequences for the future of this democracy and for our children growing up in it.

I do not want this to be about how to vote, although I have strong feelings about how not to vote and the importance of voting out theocratic candidates who would welcome a Christian America with open arms. However, I find that you can find secularists on both sides of the aisle. Certain ideologies and a true secular America are like oil and water, and even ideologies that sell well on paper will crumble under pressure from the religious movements, and both political parties are guilty of bending over backwards to accommodate this religious pressure.

The American political arena is changing quickly. Unless we are able to act, we will lose it to the religious right, and getting it back will not be as simple as voting in new powers. Once the political right gains full control, they will change any law necessary to make sure we cannot undo their gains. We are already seeing the Republican Party capitalize on this with gerrymandering laws around the country.

It is not so much a single party we need to be attacking, and while most would agree that the political right, the Republican Party, the Libertarian Party, and, of course, those affiliated with the Tea Party are the biggest threats, the problem runs deeper than simply political parties. It is the people being elected under those parties' banners that are the problem.

Too many politicians have become theocratic mouthpieces within their parties, for example, Rand Paul (R-KY), a Republican masquerading as a libertarian when convenient and a student of the selfish capitalist Ayn Rand, after whom he is so lucky to have been named. Paul seems to vote for policies without the American people in mind, without equality in mind, but always with his religion first.

In a 2010 interview with Louisville *Courier-Journal*, Paul was quoted as saying he did not think businesses should be required to serve customers of all races: "I don't like the idea of telling private business owners—I abhor racism. I think it's a bad business decision to exclude anybody from your restaurant—but, at the same time, I do believe in private ownership."[1]

What kind of message is this? There is a big difference between supporting private ownership and allowing racism to run rampant. What would happen to black families in the Deep South if all the businesses, from gas stations to grocery stores, could put up signs saying, "No Blacks"? Didn't we decide this was wrong decades ago? Yet Paul is eager to bring back segregated toilets and water fountains.

---

1   Ian Millhiser, "Rand Paul: 'The Hard Part of Believing in Freedom' Is Opposing Ban on Whites-Only Lunch Counters," ThinkProgress, May 20, 2010, accessed June 18, 2019, http://thinkprogress.org/2010/05/19/paul-civil-rights.

What do we expect from someone who believes the Civil Rights Act was wrong? Paul does not think the government has any right to tell any business or establishment how they must treat others. He later denied he had made these statements and claimed he supported the Civil Rights Act, but, unfortunately for him, his original comments are on tape.

He also believes that Christianity is under attack in the United States. He blamed the 2012 Boston Marathon bombing on a hatred of Christianity. Though the bombers made no mention of Christianity, charlatans like Paul miss no opportunity to play the victim, even while actual victims are still being treated for injuries.

Paul is a creationist and pro-life advocate. He believes private schools should replace the public school system, and he openly supports a for-profit prison system. Theocracy and money drive Rand Paul to think the way he does. This is the danger when one believes God grants rights to a person. He does not think you have your own rights, but that you have whatever rights he believes his God allows you to have. You don't have a right to an abortion, because his God says so, and you don't have a right to free quality public education, because his God, in this case money, says so.

Rand Paul is a Republican and libertarian of the worst kind, if there is, in fact, a good kind to compare him to these days. He supports the denial of individual rights and the destruction of an egalitarian society in an attempt to create a theocratic plutocracy guided solely by free-market crony capitalism.

We also must deal with the Christian dominionism of Michele Bachmann (R-MN retired), who believes America is a Christian nation chosen by God himself. She opposes marriage equality with gems such as: "If you're involved in the gay and lesbian lifestyle, it's bondage. It is personal bondage, personal despair and personal enslavement. And that's why this is so dangerous"; and "We need to have profound compassion for people who are dealing with the very real issue of sexual dysfunction in their life, and sexual identity disorders."[2] Viewing homosexuality as a mental illness is an insult to homosexuals around the world and to those who suffer from actual mental illnesses. She lacks empathy and a basic understanding of biology and society. This is the sort of vile thinking we must do our best to remove from the federal government in order to keep a liberal and progressive country in motion. Our children rely on us to make sure these types of politicians do not make laws that will someday govern their society.

Politicians like this may not be the majority, but the GOP has given them a megaphone and has allowed them to become the ambassadors of the party, mostly thanks to the Koch brothers, groups like the Heritage Foundation, the CATO Institute, and countless others who have poured millions of dollars into keeping Tea Party candidates in office, replacing moderate conservatives with extremists, and threatening those seated with tough elections if they don't get on board or at least shut up and let the Tea Party run the show. Today we're seeing the Republican Party move even further right. We have a former leader of the American Nazi Party (since rebranded the National Socialist White People's Party) winning a Republican primary.[3] We also have a Democratic Party that is now accepting pro-life candidates. There is no party on the left today. There are center-right Democrats and far-right Republicans.

---

2   Zack Ford, "Michele Bachmann's Top 10 Attacks on the LGBT Community," ThinkProgress, June 14, 2011, accessed June 21, 2019, https://thinkprogress.org/michele-bachmanns-top-10-attacks-on-the-lgbt-community-bd3534d9a681.

3   Dan Mangan, "Neo-Nazi Arthur Jones Wins Republican Nomination for Illinois Congressional Seat," *CNBC*, March 21, 2018, accessed June 21, 2019, https://www.cnbc.com/2018/03/21/neo-nazi-wins-republican-nomination-for-illinois-congressional-seat-.html.

Some slightly left Democrats want to go the progressive route. Elect slightly more left candidates every two to four years and maybe by the time our great-grandkids can vote they can actually elect a real leftist. Republicans, on the other hand, are pushing the country further right, and the further right they go, the further right the Democratic elite goes trying to chase them down and to appeal to independents. It's a losing strategy for the American people.

So now we must organize. We must look further than electoral politics to free ourselves. We should be building movements of people who take care of each other instead of looking for the next political leader to do it for us. Some of you are going to be big voting advocates, and I say more power to you, as long as you remember you also need to be in the streets fighting. You need to be building something greater than ballot boxes.

Self-Care and Protecting Yourself

Self-Care

One of the hardest things to do as a parent—and as an activist—is self-care. We spend our time at home taking care of our families and the ones we love, while out in the streets we try to help others. Those of us who have it easy in some ways tend think that we can't rest until everyone has what we have. That could not be further from the truth. You're no good to your family or your community if you're burned out.

I can't stress enough the importance to taking care of yourself. There are a few ways to do this. First, it can be as simple as just sitting something out. Big protest coming up in your town? Feeling anxious or exhausted just thinking about it? It's okay to stay home. You don't have to go if you're not feeling up to it.

You can also focus on hobbies away from activism and/or parenting. I enjoy ice hockey, video games, and movies. It's fun to do these things with my children, but I also like doing them on my own. I try my best to be fully involved in these activities to take my mind off the world. Activism is exhausting and often thankless, so you find yourself wondering why you're doing all this work and what you get out of it. When you reach that point, you're nearing burnout, and if you withdraw from activism, you're certainly not helping anyone.

You're also not helping your kids by burning out, because it often means you're spending too much time fighting the good fight and aren't spending quality time with your family. This too is problematic. While self-care does mean "taking a break" from some parenting responsibilities when you can, I often find that my biggest breaks are away from activism and are best enjoyed by spending the time with my family. Going to Disneyland, the zoo, or the local aquarium are ways we spend quality time together, and I don't think about Nazis or my Twitter account.

In the end, the issues we fight for are for our children and all the children. My children are not black, but I take part in Black Lives Matter, because I want people of color to grow up in a world different than the present one, but I also want my children to grow up in a world in which police officers aren't gunning down black lives. Sure, it doesn't affect them directly, but it affects them and all of us to varying degrees. Burning out and quitting won't help to achieve that world.

It's about knowing your limitations. It's about learning when to say stop and when to rest. It can also be about saving that energy for the bigger struggles we know we have coming. In the end, you need to do what's best for you, but you also need to do what's best for your family.

Yet it's also incredibly important that you have hobbies away from your children. We all had hobbies before kids, but often we give them up or feel we need to give them up when we become parents. You need time to yourself or with your partner away from children. Time to simply be an adult, or a kid at heart, and reconnect with your partner or yourself.

I know so many parents who feel guilty if they have fun without their kids or don't spend every free minute with them. I get it, so many of us work forty or more hours a week and feel our time with our kids is already very limited. Yet how useful or fun are you around your kids when you're just exhausted by everything? That break is for you, but it's also for them, so you can recharge and come back stronger.

Protecting Yourself

One thing you may not have thought of when you became an activist, especially if it was before kids, is protecting your identity online. If you're reading this now and thinking about getting involved, this is a great time to start thinking about the ways your identity might be accessible to others and who might use that against you.

For better or worse, I've kept a lower profile since we had our first child, although I never saw my views as controversial. I got my start debating evolution vs. creationism, and the most attention I got was from the Creation Museum's Ken Ham, who thought I was an evil "secularist." Death threats from people who think the world is six thousand years old didn't ever feel too threatening, but things changed.

I quickly learned that his followers are mean, threatening people. Then Trump was elected and fascists and Nazis took over the streets and public spaces, and I couldn't stand by and watch that happen. This led to me being doxxed, with my address published online along with links to all of my online accounts. I never actually felt my life or the lives of my family were in danger. I am a white cishet male; I can go through life without ever feeling all that threatened. That won't be the case for everyone reading this book.

There are some easy ways to protect yourself. Keep social media accounts private if you plan to share personal info, or don't share anything personal online. Perhaps keep bills in your partner's name if they are not going to be as public as you. Using a fake name on social media or in your activism is also an idea worth considering.

I chose not to, mainly because no one warned me that I might someday want to protect my real identity. It's worth remembering it can all come back on you. When I am job hunting, I know if I'm googled me, a potential employer is going to get a lot of information about me, good and bad. A lot of people don't like me and have written horrible things that are out there publicly.

With all of this comes a certain level of paranoia, some of it likely warranted, some you'll never be sure wasn't all in your head. You don't want your children to suffer any physical or mental consequences because you chose the life of an activist. While you may not worry that someone would harm your child, I can say as an out and public atheist, I do worry other parents won't let my child into their home. Of course, those aren't the kind of parents I want my child being around, but it could still take a toll on them, wondering why some kids can't play with them because of dad. Thankfully, to my knowledge, this hasn't happened yet, but I worry about it anyway.

Much like self-care, protecting yourself is something you also need to do. It's about creating a space into which you can escape. I mean escaping it all, parenting, activism, your work, you name it. You want to be able to take a break. I am grateful for what success I have had, and for me it's nice. Sure, I would have loved to have become that *New York Times* best-selling author. What author wouldn't to some degree? That hasn't happened, but I am able to write books, and that's a huge privilege. This mid-level success has perks too. I can basically go anywhere I want and not have to deal with people recognizing me very often. Sure, it happens, and I feel like a damn rock star when it does, but for the most part I am free to move around. I see celebrities on TV who can't even go grocery shopping in peace. That's a tough life.

Sure it comes with fame and fortune, but at what cost? And fame and fortune probably aren't on top of the list of things those of you reading this book are seeking to accomplish in the world.

In the end, what you're after is making change, and that can be at a smaller or greater personal cost. I hope you take a moment to think about all of the possible scenarios and about what you can do to minimize the impact on yourself or your family. Don't be discouraged from being active, but be smart about it. Go out and fight like hell to change the world but have something wonderful to come home to and something wonderful ready when you need a break for your own good.

Conclusion

The trials and tribulations of raising a child in a Christian America should not be understated. It would be easy for a Christian family not to understand the importance of this book, because they are raising children as part of the majority. They will not face discrimination for their religious beliefs. Even if laws are changed to favor equality and reinforce the separation of church and state, believers will not face persecution, though they likely disagree with this, as the religious right does seem to have the world's largest persecution complex.

The truth is, any persecution or discrimination lies solely on their side. The laws the religious right wishes to pass would discriminate against women, LGBTQ citizens, and atheists. They even support political parties that would discriminate against racialized minorities.

Part of raising children is raising them to carry on our legacy, and our legacy is creating a better world. A better world cannot be created through religious dogma, oppression, or discrimination. Success will come through the secularization of this country and the furthering of equality. When it comes to secularization, many religions see this as the opposite of theocracy. It is not, and we should work on better educating the public. Secularism means equal rights and protection for all religious beliefs and for those without religious beliefs. In a theocracy, one religion rules the land, while secularism treats all religions equally.

Our success in further secularizing America will be achieved by raising freethinkers, as well as by our actions and by changing the hearts and minds of those with whom we engage. Change doesn't happen overnight; the battle we pass on to our children will be far from over when we leave this world, and it is one they will most likely be passing on to their children. It would be beautiful to think that the U.S. or the world could change in a single generation, but the truth is we have lots of work ahead of us. Even if we managed to accomplish all our goals tomorrow, there is a whole world of oppression waiting to be fixed.

We find ourselves in a unique position. Many of us are part of the first generation of parents who can be so open and vocal about our atheism, and while this does not hold true for the entire country, we are getting there. We have the ability to organize as atheists, skeptics, freethinkers, and secularists and to work toward policy change and toward shifting the direction of this country.

We must be careful not to raise puppets that just do as we say; our children should question us. I feel the fight I am a part of is important, and I believe I am on the side of right, but our children may come to learn things that we believe are wrong are, in fact, correct. As our understanding of things like well-being becomes clearer, we may find we have been wrong about a number of issues, just as was the case for previous generations.

Imagine an America where we did not learn from the mistakes of those before us or question their actions. Slavery might still be legal, women might be denied the right to vote, and all fifty states could be executing criminals. While we have made great progress, it is no secret that we have yet far to go. I will feel we've succeeded when all states have banned capital punishment, when the prisons are empty, and when laws are passed for the right reasons, not because some politicians believe that God's law is the law of the land.

I could go on and on about when I will declare victories, and I hope that throughout my lifetime I will have the chance to claim many, but I also know that for each success, there are hundreds more issues ahead of us. Regardless of this daunting realization, I am inspired by the progress we have made.

This book is my appeal to parents to be more involved, not only in your child's life but as an atheist in your community, at the PTA, on the school board, in local politics, and, of course, to some degree, even in national politics. Make your voice heard, and make sure your concerns are addressed. Do not accept being brushed aside as a minority. The Christian right is making their power grab, and it will be up to those of us who cannot stand for a theocratic America to stand up and be the opposition. If we don't do it, who will?

When I sat down to begin writing this book, I thought it would be a book about how to teach your kids about religion and science, but as I wrote I realized there is so much more to parenting as a nonbeliever than religion and science. You cannot ignore politics, and you can't bypass addressing death, sex, and the meaning of life. I saw this book morph quickly, in line with the political climate.

I wanted to turn my inspiration into words that would resonate and hopefully motivate at least one other person to get up, go out there, and make a difference. Maybe this person is sitting at home with no idea what they can do. Maybe this person is active but wants to do more. Maybe this person is fed up with the lack of effective change and doesn't think they can make a difference.

If this person is you, know this: you can make a difference, you will make a difference, and you should strive to make a difference.

You may put this book down and disagree with my tactics or my politics, but my hope is that you also put it down feeling inspired to make change. You may think I am nothing more than another opinionated anarchist, or you may think I am too hard on religion or that coming out is not right for you and your family, but I know that you will have found something in this book to light a fire under you. When it comes to science education, maybe you didn't think to really check not only what they are teaching in your child's science class but what they are not teaching. My parents knew what I was being taught, but I don't think it dawned on them in many cases to figure out what I was not being taught.

I often wonder if my life would have been different had I been introduced to Darwin much sooner and if my schools had not simply ignored his contributions to science. I wonder, if my history classes had been more honest about the founding of our country, the reasons we got involved in foreign wars, and had been more open about politics in general, whether I would have had a different political view much earlier. I think back to my schooling; I never learned about Marx and Engels, never heard of Lenin or Trotsky. I understand a high school student may not need to know much about this, but to know nothing about some of the people who had an impact on our whole world is surely not right. If someone like Lenin was mentioned, it was only as an evil dictator, and communism was going to ruin the world.

Teaching our children the truth is extremely important, even if it makes our country look bad. We cannot skirt around slavery and just focus on how we freed the slaves. Yes, we freed the slaves, but we are also responsible for enslaving them. We did watch *Roots* in my school,[1] but we really didn't discuss it. We watched it over the course of a week or so and never had a good discussion about it. I remember kids in my class laughing at scenes, because it just didn't feel real. How could it be? How could this story be real in the United States?

---

1   Marvin J. Chomsky, John Erman, David Greene, and Gilbert Moses, dirs., *Roots*, parts 1–8 (Burbank, CA: ABC, 1977).

Yet it is, and it's scary. We act like heroes for freeing the slaves, but half the country is still upset about it.

One thing is certain; the Christian right is abusing our political and educational systems and our children. They are fighting to put an end to secularization and will stop at nothing short of an American theocracy. I wrote this book because I cannot let that happen, and I do not want my children to grow up in that kind of country. Instead of packing my bags, I am taking action, and I am asking you to do the same.

As parents, we can no longer stand by and think the world is just going to get better. It only gets better when people make it that way. This fight started long before us, and it will live on after us. We can pass the torch on to our children if, when that time comes, the fight still needs to be fought. In raising children eager and ready to think for themselves, we ensure that they will not walk the streets as part of the brainwashed masses taking orders from the pulpit. They will question authority and use evidence and reason as their guide, instead of fear and greed.

So, with that, I urge you to come out and be an active member in your community, be proud of who you are, and show your children, by example, that we should not hide who we are. We have a lot of work to do, and I look forward to doing it with you.

Acknowledgments

It should go without saying that this book would not have been possible without my family. My wife Danielle and our two amazing children inspired this book and inspire me every day.

Thanks to my parents for allowing me to grow up a free-thinker and for never holding me back from exploring the religions of the world.

Finally, a thank you to everyone at PM Press for making this book possible, as well as a special thank you to Kurt Volkan from Pitchstone Publishing. Without his generosity, you wouldn't be reading this right now.

Index

"Passim" (literally "scattered") indicates intermittent discussion of a topic over a cluster of pages.

About the Authors

Dan Arel lives in California with his family. He is a freelance columnist, author, and labor advocate. His work has appeared in a number of publications, including *Time*, Huffington Post, AlterNet, Salon, *The Hill*, and *The New Arab*.

He is the recipient of the 2014 American Atheists First Amendment Award for Investigative Journalism for his work helping to expose the Ark Encounter, a Noah's Ark theme park that received millions of dollars in tax incentives from the Commonwealth of Kentucky.

Jessica Mills is a touring musician, artist, activist, writer, teacher, and mother. She is author of *My Mother Wears Combat Boots: A Parenting Guide for the Rest of Us*.

ABOUT PM PRESS

PM Press was founded at the end of 2007 by a small collection of folks with decades of publishing, media, and organizing experience. PM Press co-conspirators have published and distributed hundreds of books, pamphlets, CDs, and DVDs. Members of PM have founded enduring book fairs, spearheaded victorious tenant organizing campaigns, and worked closely with bookstores, academic conferences, and even rock bands to deliver political and challenging ideas to all walks of life. We're old enough to know what we're doing and young enough to know what's at stake.

We seek to create radical and stimulating fiction and nonfiction books, pamphlets, T-shirts, visual and audio materials to entertain, educate, and inspire you. We aim to distribute these through every available channel with every available technology—whether that means you are seeing anarchist classics at our bookfair stalls, reading our latest vegan cookbook at the café, downloading geeky fiction e-books, or digging new music and timely videos from our website.

PM Press is always on the lookout for talented and skilled volunteers, artists, activists, and writers to work with. If you have a great idea for a project or can contribute in some way, please get in touch.

PM Press
PO Box 23912
Oakland, CA 94623
www.pmpress.org

PM Press in Europe
europe@pmpress.org
www.pmpress.org.uk

FRIENDS OF PM PRESS

These are indisputably momentous times—the
financial system is melting down globally and
the Empire is stumbling. Now more than ever
there is a vital need for radical ideas.

In the years since its founding—and on a
mere shoestring—PM Press has risen to the formidable challenge
of publishing and distributing knowledge and entertainment for the
struggles ahead. With over 300 releases to date, we have published an
impressive and stimulating array of literature, art, music, politics, and
culture. Using every available medium, we've succeeded in connecting
those hungry for ideas and information to those putting them into
practice.

Friends of PM allows you to directly help impact, amplify, and revitalize
the discourse and actions of radical writers, filmmakers, and artists. It
provides us with a stable foundation from which we can build upon our
early successes and provides a much-needed subsidy for the materials
that can't necessarily pay their own way. You can help make that
happen—and receive every new title automatically delivered to your
door once a month—by joining as a Friend of PM Press. And, we'll throw
in a free T-shirt when you sign up.

Here are your options:

- **$30 a month** Get all books and pamphlets plus 50% discount on all
  webstore purchases

- **$40 a month** Get all PM Press releases (including CDs and DVDs)
  plus 50% discount on all webstore purchases

- **$100 a month** Superstar—Everything plus PM merchandise, free
  downloads, and 50% discount on all webstore purchases

For those who can't afford $30 or more a month, we have **Sustainer
Rates** at $15, $10 and $5. Sustainers get a free PM Press T-shirt and a
50% discount on all purchases from our website.

Your Visa or Mastercard will be billed once a month, until you tell us to
stop. Or until our efforts succeed in bringing the revolution around. Or
the financial meltdown of Capital makes plastic redundant. Whichever
comes first.

Godless: 150 Years of Disbelief

Chaz Bufe
with an Introduction by Dan Arel

ISBN: 978-1-62963-641-2
$19.95   224 pages

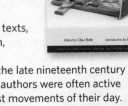

Godless is a compilation of wide-ranging texts, both hilarious and horrifying, on atheism, belief, and religion. The selections in the book appeared in various formats from the late nineteenth century through the early twenty-first, and their authors were often active in the anarchist, Marxist, or radical leftist movements of their day. Derived from printed pamphlets, books by small publishers, and essays that appeared in widely distributed newspapers, these texts serve as freethinking propaganda in a media war against morbid authoritarian doctrines.

With both a sophisticated analysis of inconsistencies in deistic beliefs and a biting satirical edge, *Godless* gives ammunition to those fighting fundamentalist bigotry—and more than a few reasons to abandon Christianity.

Readers previously familiar with the authors' political polemics will be rewarded in contemplating another side of their remarkable literary output. Contributors include Emma Goldman, Ambrose Bierce, Chaz Bufe, E. Haldeman-Julius, Earl Lee, Johann Most, Joseph McCabe, Matilda Gage, Pamela Sutter, S.C. Hitchcock, and Sébastien Faure.

"The book is a far-reaching collection of timeless, provocative, politically astute quotations from a wide range of people active in many walks of life. It is fun, informative, and more."
—*Z Magazine*, on *The Heretic's Handbook of Quotations*

"Such bitterness, such negativity, such unbridled humor, wit and sarcasm."
—*Mensa Bulletin* on *The American Heretic's Dictionary*

"No serious scholar of Catholicism can afford to miss the McCabe reprints. Less serious readers may be entertained by his erudite asides and vituperative language."
—Donald Rooum, *Freedom Fortnightly*

Revolutionary Mothering: Love on the Front Lines

Edited by Alexis Pauline Gumbs,
China Martens, and Mai'a Williams
with a preface by Loretta J. Ross

ISBN: 978-1-62963-110-3
$17.95   272 pages

Inspired by the legacy of radical and queer
black feminists of the 1970s and '80s,
Revolutionary Mothering places marginalized mothers of color at the
center of a world of necessary transformation. The challenges we face as
movements working for racial, economic, reproductive, gender, and food
justice, as well as anti-violence, anti-imperialist, and queer liberation
are the same challenges that many mothers face every day. Oppressed
mothers create a generous space for life in the face of life-threatening
limits, activate a powerful vision of the future while navigating tangible
concerns in the present, move beyond individual narratives of choice
toward collective solutions, live for more than ourselves, and remain
accountable to a future that we cannot always see. *Revolutionary
Mothering* is a movement-shifting anthology committed to birthing new
worlds, full of faith and hope for what we can raise up together.

Contributors include June Jordan, Malkia A. Cyril, Esteli Juarez, Cynthia
Dewi Oka, Fabiola Sandoval, Sumayyah Talibah, Victoria Law, Tara
Villalba, Lola Mondragón, Christy NaMee Eriksen, Norma Angelica
Marrun, Vivian Chin, Rachel Broadwater, Autumn Brown, Layne Russell,
Noemi Martinez, Katie Kaput, alba onofrio, Gabriela Sandoval, Cheryl
Boyce Taylor, Ariel Gore, Claire Barrera, Lisa Factora-Borchers, Fabielle
Georges, H. Bindy K. Kang, Terri Nilliasca, Irene Lara, Panquetzani,
Mamas of Color Rising, tk karakashian tunchez, Arielle Julia Brown,
Lindsey Campbell, Micaela Cadena, and Karen Su.

*"This collection is a treat for anyone that sees class and that needs to learn
more about the experiences of women of color (and who doesn't?!). There
is no dogma here, just fresh ideas and women of color taking on capitalism,
anti-racist, anti-sexist theory-building that is rooted in the most primal
of human connections, the making of two people from the body of one:
mothering."*
—Barbara Jensen, author of *Reading Classes: On Culture and Classism in
America*

Rad Families: A Celebration

Edited by Tomas Moniz
with a Foreword by Ariel Gore

ISBN: 978-1-62963-230-8
$19.95   296 pages

Rad Families: A Celebration honors the messy,
the painful, the playful, the beautiful, the
myriad ways we create families. This is not
an anthology of experts, or how-to articles on
perfect parenting; it often doesn't even try to
provide answers. Instead, the writers strive to be honest and vulnerable
in sharing their stories and experiences, their failures and their regrets.

Gathering parents and writers from diverse communities, it explores
the process of getting pregnant from trans birth to adoption, grapples
with issues of racism and police brutality, probes raising feminists and
feminist parenting. It plumbs the depths of empty nesting and letting go.

Some contributors are recognizable authors and activists but most are
everyday parents working and loving and trying to build a better world
one diaper change at a time. It's a book that reminds us all that we are
not alone, that community can help us get through the difficulties, can,
in fact, make us better people. It's a celebration, join us!

Contributors include Jonas Cannon, Ian MacKaye, Burke Stansbury,
Danny Goot, Simon Knaphus, Artnoose, Welch Canavan, Daniel Muro
LaMere, Jennifer Lewis, Zach Ellis, Alicia Dornadic, Jesse Palmer, Mindi
J., Carla Bergman, Tasnim Nathoo, Rachel Galindo, Robert Liu-Trujillo,
Dawn Caprice, Shawn Taylor, D.A. Begay, Philana Dollin, Airial Clark,
Allison Wolfe, Roger Porter, cubbie rowland-storm, Annakai & Rob
Geshlider, Jeremy Adam Smith, Frances Hardinge, Jonathan Shipley,
Bronwyn Davies Glover, Amy Abugo Ongiri, Mike Araujo, Craig Elliott,
Eleanor Wohlfeiler, Scott Hoshida, Plinio Hernandez, Madison Young,
Nathan Torp, Sasha Vodnik, Jessie Susannah, Krista Lee Hanson, Carvell
Wallace, Dani Burlison, Brian Whitman, scott winn, Kermit Playfoot,
Chris Crass, and Zora Moniz.

*"Rad dads, rad families, rad children. These stories show us that we are not
alone. That we don't have all the answers. That we are all learning."*
—Nikki McClure, illustrator, author, parent

"Rad Families *is the collection for all families."*
—Innosanto Nagara, author/illustrator of *A Is for Activist*

Rad Dad: Dispatches from the Frontiers of Fatherhood

Edited by Jeremy Adam Smith and Tomas Moniz

ISBN: 978-1-60486-481-6
$15.00   200 pages

Rad Dad: Dispatches from the Frontiers of Fatherhood combines the best pieces from the award-winning zine *Rad Dad* and from the blog Daddy Dialectic, two kindred publications that have tried to explore parenting as political territory. Both of these projects have pushed the conversation around fathering beyond the safe, apolitical focus most books and websites stick to; they have not been complacent but have worked hard to create a diverse, multi-faceted space in which to grapple with the complexity of fathering. Today more than ever, fatherhood demands constant improvisation, risk, and struggle. With grace and honesty and strength, *Rad Dad*'s writers tackle all the issues that other parenting guides are afraid to touch: the brutalities, beauties, and politics of the birth experience, the challenges of parenting on an equal basis with mothers, the tests faced by transgendered and gay fathers, the emotions of sperm donation, and parental confrontations with war, violence, racism, and incarceration. *Rad Dad* is for every father out in the real world trying to parent in ways that are loving, meaningful, authentic, and ultimately revolutionary.

Contributors include: Steve Almond, Jack Amoureux, Mike Araujo, Mark Andersen, Jeff Chang, Ta-Nehisi Coates, Jeff Conant, Sky Cosby, Jason Denzin, Cory Doctorow, Craig Elliott, Chip Gagnon, Keith Hennessy, David L. Hoyt, Simon Knapus, Ian MacKaye, Tomas Moniz, Zappa Montag, Raj Patel, Jeremy Adam Smith, Jason Sperber, Burke Stansbury, Shawn Taylor, Tata, Jeff West, and Mark Whiteley.

"Rad Dad gives voice to egalitarian parenting and caregiving by men in a truly radical fashion, with its contributors challenging traditional norms of what it means to be a father and subverting paradigms, while making you laugh in the process. With its thoughtful and engaging stories on topics like birth, stepfathering, gender, politics, pop culture, and the challenges of kids growing older, this collection of essays and interviews is a compelling addition to books on fatherhood."
—Jennifer Silverman, co-editor, *My Baby Rides the Short Bus: The Unabashedly Human Experience of Raising Kids with Disabilities*

This Is How We Survive: Revolutionary Mothering, War, and Exile in the 21st Century

Mai'a Williams
with a Foreword by Ariel Gore

ISBN: 978-1-62963-556-9
$17.95   224 pages

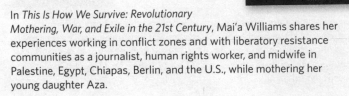

In *This Is How We Survive: Revolutionary Mothering, War, and Exile in the 21st Century*, Mai'a Williams shares her experiences working in conflict zones and with liberatory resistance communities as a journalist, human rights worker, and midwife in Palestine, Egypt, Chiapas, Berlin, and the U.S., while mothering her young daughter Aza.

She first went to Palestine in 2003 during the Second Intifada to support Palestinians resisting the Israeli occupation. In 2006, she became pregnant in Bethlehem, West Bank. By the time her daughter was three years old, they had already celebrated with Zapatista women in southern Mexico and survived Israeli detention, and during the 2011 Arab Spring they were in the streets of Cairo protesting the Mubarak dictatorship. She watched the Egyptian revolution fall apart and escaped the violence, like many of her Arab comrades, by moving to Europe. Three years later, she and Aza were camping at Standing Rock in protest of the Dakota Access Pipeline and co-creating revolutionary mothering communities once again.

This is a story about mothers who are doing the work of deep social transformation by creating the networks of care that sustain movements and revolutions. By centering mothers in our organizing work, we center those who have the skills and the experience of creating and sustaining life on this planet. *This Is How We Survive* illuminates how mothering is a practice essential to the work of revolution. It explores the heartbreak of revolutionary movements falling apart and revolutionaries scattering across the globe into exile. And most importantly, how mamas create, no matter the conditions, the resilience to continue doing revolutionary work.

"This is How We Survive *redefines revolution beyond the headline grabbing events to the everyday resilience of families living under ever-present threats of bombings, assaults, arrests and disappearances. This book will push you to expand and reimagine your definitions and ideas of revolution.*"
—Victoria Law, author of *Resistance Behind Bars*

Birth Work as Care Work: Stories from Activist Birth Communities

Alana Apfel, with a foreword by Loretta J. Ross, preface by Victoria Law, and introduction by Silvia Federici

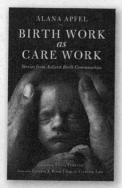

ISBN: 978-1-62963-151-6
$14.95   128 pages

Birth Work as Care Work presents a vibrant collection of stories and insights from the front lines of birth activist communities. The personal has once more become political, and birth workers, supporters, and doulas now find themselves at the fore of collective struggles for freedom and dignity.

The author, herself a scholar and birth justice organiser, provides a unique platform to explore the political dynamics of birth work; drawing connections between birth, reproductive labor, and the struggles of caregiving communities today. Articulating a politics of care work in and through the reproductive process, the book brings diverse voices into conversation to explore multiple possibilities and avenues for change.

At a moment when agency over our childbirth experiences is increasingly centralized in the hands of professional elites, *Birth Work as Care Work* presents creative new ways to reimagine the trajectory of our reproductive processes. Most importantly, the contributors present new ways of thinking about the entire life cycle, providing a unique and creative entry point into the essence of all human struggle—the struggle over the reproduction of life itself.

"I love this book, all of it. The polished essays and the interviews with birth workers dare to take on the deepest questions of human existence."
—Carol Downer, cofounder of the Feminist Women's Heath Centers of California and author of *A Woman's Book of Choices*

"This volume provides theoretically rich, practical tools for birth and other care workers to collectively and effectively fight capitalism and the many intersecting processes of oppression that accompany it. Birth Work as Care Work forcefully and joyfully reminds us that the personal is political, a lesson we need now more than ever."
—Adrienne Pine, author of *Working Hard, Drinking Hard: On Violence and Survival in Honduras*